Releasing the
IMPOSSIBLE

The Limitless Power of Intercession

VOLUME ONE

By Jeanne Metcalf

Copyright © 2000

Third Edition
Cëgullah Publishing
International Copyright © 2022
www.cegullahpublishing.ca

All rights reserved

Volume 1: ISBN 978-1-926489-45-2
Volume 2: ISBN 978-1-926489-46-9
Workbook: ISBN 978-1-926489-03-2

(Workbook covers both Volumes)

Cover photo ©istock.com

Cover design by Jeanne Metcalf.

COPYRIGHT MATTERS

This book is an original manuscript by the author, protected by international copyright laws of Canada. Therefore, none of this author's work may be reproduced, in part or in whole, or stored in a retrieval system, or transmitted in any form or by any means, electronic, mechanical, photocopied, recorded or otherwise for commercial use without the *prior written* permission of the author. However, it is possible to receive permission to use short quotations for personal use, or use in a group study, or for permission to copy certain passages, or to make portions of the writings available for overhead viewing. Simply, contact the author[1] to request it.

All scripture quotes originate from KJV[2], public domain. However, the name of God appears as YeHoVaH, not LORD. See appendix for more information.

---

[1] To contact author, see *Contact Page in Appendix*

[2] KJV refers to all humankind as "man". Unless the passage itself refers to a particular male person, apply the message to all humankind, regardless of gender.

CHARACTERS IN THE BOOK

Releasing the Impossible records true events and are written to the best of the author's ability to recall them. Individuals mentioned in this book are real but given fictitious names, other than the name of Jeanne's husband and their only son[3]. Since it has been more than 20 years since this book was initially written, it is possible that, today, the characters spoken about within the book might recollect the events differently. Should this occur, first note that Jeanne wrote these stories from an intercessor's point of view, and thus the individuals involved were not priviledged to hear, see or realize the behind the scene events in her life s they took place.

Secondly, Jeanne was not physically present in all places where these events took place, but received only the information by spiritual insight. Lastly, remember that the intent of this book is to reveal intercession's power, therefore, no malicious intent was intended toward any individual mentioned in the book, *(real name or fictitious),* for in the eyes of God and His servant, individuals are perceived in the best light possible, regardless of the issues with which they struggle. In intercession, no individual is ever condemned or seen in a negative light. As a reader, we ask you to extend that same loving mindset to the characters and their life happenings recorded within the book.

---

[3] Jeanne received permission to use their real names as no conflict of viewpoint occurred at the initial writing of the book in the year 2000.

DEDICATION

Once again, with heartfelt gratitude, I dedicate Releasing the Impossible, now in its third edition. I give all the thanks and glory to my Teacher and Partner in Intercession, Yeshua Ha' Maschiach.

In addition, I honour my husband, Gary, who tremendously encouraged me in my calling for over forty years now. Also, as in the dedication of the first edition of the book, I make honourable mention of my parents, who encouraged me I wrote the first edition of this book. Their labours of love in my life will never be forgotten, even though they live, now, in eternity.

IN THIS BOOK
Volume 1: ISBN 978-1-926489-45-2[4]

*This Volume contains stories of intercession **completed by the author**. Each story selected shows a type of intercession, aligning it with Biblical principles.*

TABLE OF CONTENTS

	Why Two Volumes	9
	Introduction	11
1	Before Intercession	15
2	Agony and Ecstasy of Intercession	23
	Part A 23	
	Part B 37	
	Part C 55	
3	The Shocking Reality of Visions	69
4	Impending Danger Strikes Out	89
5	Captured by YeHoVaH's Love	117
6	Carried on Majestic Wings	147
7	Into the Realms of Glory	179

---

[4] *It works best to complete Volume 1 before attempting to do Volume 2.*

APPENDIX

About the Author	224
About the King James Version	203
A Name to Honour	197
Contact Information	224
Intercessory Types Defined	212
Jonah's Situational Intercession	205
No Formulas for Success	204
Other books by Jeanne Metcalf	222
Principles of Intercession by Number	210
Salvation Message	215
Scripture Index	220
Sinner's Prayer & Commitment	218

CHART INDEX

An Intercession's Basic Components	34
Intercession Principle Recaps:	
Agony & Ecstasy of Intercession	37
Shocking Reality of Visions	76
Impending Danger Strikes Out	101
Captured by YeHoVaH's Love	129
Carried on Majestic Wings	163
Into the Realms of Glory	187
Jonah's Intercession Principle Recap	205

WHY TWO VOLUMES

When the first printing of Releasing the Impossible became available to readers, many desired to use the material as a Bible Study. To comply, I divided the course into segments, with one chapter taught and discussed per week. While this helped the students to ingest the material, however, due to the number of chapters, it required a lengthy time commitment by both teacher and student. Some found that time commitment difficult.

Therefore, dividing "Releasing the Impossible" into two volumes, seemed a good solution. With two volumes, each one becoming a separate Bible Study, teachers and students have opportunity for a shorter commitment, and can also implement a break in between. This solution, therefore, makes sense as people can learn at a slower rate, and thus, walk away with a far greater understanding.

At least, this is my prayer and hope.

Please Note:

***** **Volume 1 must be read first.** *****

FROM THE AUTHOR

In the year 2000, the Holy Spirit encouraged me to author this book entitled, Releasing the Impossible. While I have written many more books since this one, the other books explore the Word of God from a teaching perspective[5], without personal input such as found in this book.

Releasing the Impossible, my very first book, stands alone in sharing the deep personal treasures of my heart. Those experiences present a testimony to the greatness of our God. Additionally, by laying those intercessory experiences out before His people, it gives others opportunity to understand and then enjoy the same power in intercession as the Holy Spirit taught me.

As you read this book, please realize the heart of sharing it! It is not a book to boast of one person's accomplishments. If you see that in the book, then the whole purpose of authoring the book lays buried. Releasing the Impossible stretches out *to you* an invitation to join the Living God so that you can tap into the limitless power of Intercession. Please see this as the heart of this book and reach out to God to experience great intercessory accomplishments for God!

Many thanks for doing that and blessings, also

---

[5] See Other books by other to read the list of available materials.

INTRODUCTION

Throughout my Christian experience, YeHoVaH has schooled me in the subject of intercession. He then instructed me to teach others. I have done as He asked of me, with very positive results. In fact, those I taught wanted the information available in a book form. The question was then, how to do that? For me lesson notes were easily prepared, but to write a book constitutes so many unknowns.

Also in a classroom setting, I can see the faces! To ease the mind of a puzzled student, I can stop teaching and explain any point I skipped over too quickly but to write a book is another story. I had so many uncertainties to face! How could I be sure the reader will fully understand the topic as I presented it?

How could I ensure the book would be self-explanatory and not a manual in need of a teacher to explain it? Indeed, how could I convey my passionate desire for everyone to walk arm in arm with YeHoVaH so they could discover the depths of intercession and

Introduction

be encouraged to explore and share the wonderful world of intercession?

With tenacity and trust in YeHoVaH, I decided if I "could" write a book it would *touch more people than a classroom,* or any one-on-one encounter. After ions of prayer, encouragement, and many hours, too numerous to mention, I finally wrote the book with a prime directive to keep it simple, easily grasped by beginners and valued by intermediate and experienced intercessors as well. To present this book, in what I hope is a clear, concise, and enjoyable format, I decided to divide the book into books.

VOLUME 1:
This section includes specific stories of intercessions taken from my personal experience. After relating the stories, I then highlight the biblical principles at work in them.

VOLUME 2:
This section records stories of intercession straight from the Bible. Here I re-enforce the principles learned earlier in Section One, then I introduce new principles not yet discussed. The last section explains a valuable principle for believers to establish a consistent life of intercession.

The Appendix:
The Appendix of both volumes recaps and categorizes all the principles mentioned and gives a definition of the types of intercession as well.

With this format, I trust that I have adequately illustrated, detailed, and expounded these spiritual truths about intercession. One last thing to mention is that to ensure the book is clear and effective, I taught a course on intercession *using this material*. In this way, I was able to measure the educational benefits and effectiveness of the book, along with the student's comments and reactions. As a direct result of that course on intercession:

1. new intercessors, with a heart to learn, boldly entered intercession.
2. experienced intercessors found greater depth to their intercessory activities.
3. tired intercessors found new vigour and zeal.
4. and intercessors, stalled for a season, found a springboard to escalate them to new heights in the realms of prayer.

In short, the students were positioned on a course of transformation to become greater and mightier in the realms of intercession. How awesome!

In addition to the proof of changed lives, students openly expressed their appreciation for the material and wished it had been available earlier. They encouraged me to "hurry up" and publish the book. Then YeHoVaH validated the book when the proof reader, a relatively new intercessor, read the book and received an anointing for intercession that took her to new heights with YeHoVaH.

This is my desire for you too, that your prayer life will be transformed by the power of the Holy Spirit. As He pours His Holy Spirit upon you, may your heart be drawn closer and closer to Him. May He whisk you away to places of intimacy with Him where your entire being will be fully satisfied. May your skills in intercession soar to new heights, to delight both your heart and YeHoVaH!

Please remember, also, dear reader, that this book gives a personal account of intercession, highlighting my intercessor giftings but with a purpose to show you what is available to all! As you read this book, please only hear the heart of a servant sharing to help others soar with God. Keep foremost in you mind that God is no respecter[6] of persons. What He does for one, He does for others! May these words encourage you to press in for all God has for you!

---

[6] Acts 10:34

BEFORE INTERCESSION

There is a place, near the heart of YeHoVaH, where every believer is invited to come. That special place echoes with His Holiness; reveals the warmth of His Presence, the Tendnerness of His Embrace and the Radiance of His Love. This is the place of His Glory, the place where we are tucked safely away in the cleft of the rock, covered with His Hand.

This place summons every believer, but it takes a journey to reach the destination. No one arrives in an instant. There are no overnight success stories. This place is obtained by faith as we walk step by step towards it. This place of intimacy with YeHoVaH and its journey is a process that is part of the believer's destiny.

It begins the moment we seriously embark on our excursion to truly know YeHoVaH. As we pursue Him, every step we take will bring us closer and closer to that holy and sure place where we encounter His glory, but that place of intimacy with YeHoVaH has a price tag.

While there is no need to pay any further price towards our salvation, there is a *personal price* to pay for *intimacy with* YeHoVaH. Every believer has the ability to pay the price, but to do so means relinquishing our control, yielding and totally surrendering every aspect of our life to the Holy Spirit. The price tag includes personal and spiritual discipline, sacrifice of self-interest, and in fact, total abandoment to self. These things and more are part and parcel of the cost a believer pays to know YeHoVaH intimately, but after all, anything we value to a great extent, will cost us.

On this earth, there is no greater treasure than to know its Creator personally and thoroughly and the price tag for that relationship matches it value. For those who pay the price, the rewards of the relationship with the Master far outweigh the cost, and in fact, far surpass anything else this world has to offer. That intimate place with YeHoVaH will marinate the soul with knowledge of Him and produce a satisfying and fulfilling relationship, but it does not come cheap.

In my life, the marinating process, infusing the knowledge of YeHoVaH into my being, has taken well over 20 years, and of course, has come with a price tag. Both process and price tag were wrapped up in the neat little packages of life's lessons that YeHoVaH taught me.

In my opinion, these lessons were taught at very inconvenient times and went on far too long. Many lessons seemed too difficult for me to manage and I wondered why I had to learn these lessons at all! I could neither see, nor appreciate their importance *at the time*, but eventually it became apparent that each lesson had a value hidden beneath the surface. The hardest lessons, the ones I struggled with the most, were the ones that required me to totally abandon my own desires and forsake my quests to fulfill my deepest dreams. The lessons learned at the greatest personal cost ended up to be the lessons of the deepest worth, *revealing the Divine and Holy character of* YeHoVaH, *exposing to me His deepest Desires and the quests that would obtain His Dreams.*

As YeHoVaH began to reveal these things to me, as He came closer through every lesson, I discovered a certain humility that He emitted whenever I was in His Presence; hard to explain, but wonderful to experience. I saw the passions of His Heart; the treasures He pursued; what He longed for. I learned to rest in the righteousness of His Choices, and eventually, after accepting His full claim on my life, I saw great effectiveness of His methods. I began to grip what it really meant to know Him.

Receiving more revelation brought His amazing qualities to light. The more alive He became to me, and the more I understood His character, I recognized my obvious lack of it. Every circumstance, every situation, every incident that touched my life afforded opportunities for His character to be forged in me. Every moment of every day became one more adventure to know Him, but again, each encounter had a purpose, a lesson to be learned in this classroom of life.

As with all education, there is a unique direction, a focus to the training, a *"major" or "specialty"* in your training. This major or specialty is usually the "pivot" or "center" of your career. Educational development with YeHoVaH takes a lifetime and although graduation day is not until we leave for the realms of glory, we can have a major or specialty in our training that we constantly use while on earth. My "major" or "specialty" placed certain keys in my hand. These keys helped me to understand how to release YeHoVaH's Power, so that His plans and purposes would be fulfilled on this earth. My major was, and still is, "intercession".

I was introduced to intercession in the early months of my Christian experience, at a time when I was feeling overwhelmed and desperate. My only son, five years old, was given a diagnosis that offered no hope for his survival. During this darkened hour, when my heart was breaking and my mind was drowning in emotional torrents, YeHoVaH encouraged me to press in closer to His heart to discover His Intentions. Once discovered, I found His will for my son was "life" and not "death".

It was at that point, I was introduced to the power and benefit of intercession. The Holy Spirit taught me to take hold of YeHoVaH, to move into the realms of faith, and then He showed me some basic principles to release His Plans and Purposes into the desperate situation. *As a direct result of that intercession,* I saw the prognosis of my son's death reversed, and furthermore, witnessed my son's full and complete restoration.

From then onward, intercession would play a large part in my life. With awe, I would watch YeHoVaH repeatedly, through the avenue of intercession, turn hopeless situations into testimonies to His greatness. The Holy Spirit, my faithful Teacher and Mentor, planned every assignment of intercession carefully, walking with me every step of the way. He taught me very effective principles of intercession that operate throughout various types of intercession.

These types and principles, I would like to share with you.

This book then, explains intercession types and major principles that generate intercession. This book is not intended to contain everything about intercession. My intentions are not to write an encyclopaedia on the subject, nor to put intercession into little theological boxes either.

My purpose is to share precious experiences in intercession that *expose* YeHoVaH's character, so that you, dear reader, can grasp the depths of intercession and at the same time, discover a greater knowledge of YeHoVaH, understanding more completely His availability to you and your need. Consequently, your relationship with Him will grow through every intercession you do, for it is only from that relationship that you will understand how to trigger His Power. Once His Power is released, there follows a fruit from your times of intercession: *the fulfillment of the plans and purposes of* YeHoVaH.

It is my prayer that Yeshua Ha' Mashiach opens the world of intercession to you. Any blindfold of doubt that *He may see,* I pray He will remove, and if need be, apply His eye salve to your eyes, so you can clearly recognize the door that leads to intercession, and boldly walk through it. If you already have walked through the door to intercession, may He increase your depth and take you on journeys that far surpass your wildest dreams.

True delights await both teacher and student as the benefits of intercession are explained, expounded, and experienced. It is my prayer each reader will encounter the fullest revelation of YeHoVaH's Character; will taste His menu of delights as He unveils the limitless power of intercession; and then by Him, through Him, in Him, and for Him, will release the impossible into situations to afford Him great glory, honour and praise.

AGONY & ECSTASY OF INTERCESSION

PART A

Anyone who has lost a child, or has even come close to losing one, will tell you that it is a devastating experience. The very thought of your child's death brings a lump into your throat and a sick feeling into the pit of your stomach. I remember every emotion I experienced when the doctors told me my five-year-old son, Steve, would not make it through the night. Moment by moment, I agonized through what seemed like an eternity.

Various emotions churned mercilessly within me as I struggled to make sense of it all. I just wanted the ordeal over and with a happy ending. Desperation engulfed me. Thoughts bombarded my mind with questions such as: "Why did this happen? How could

YeHoVaH allow my only child to die?" I examined every detail of the events that led up to that moment and aggressively probed them for some clues to answer my many questions.

As I recalled the events, my mind went back to a week earlier. My husband Gary, our son Steve and I were invited to be part of a family holiday with my parents at a summer cottage on a lake approximately 45 minutes from our home. Although my husband declined the offer to go, choosing instead to stay behind and take care of some unfinished business, Steve and I accepted the invitation to enjoy the summer sun. I packed the car with holiday supplies, and we travelled to the lake with my husband's blessing.

When we arrived at our destination, my parents were waiting for us. Excitedly, they came to the car and greeted us. This promised to be a wonderful, intimate family time! When Steve saw the lake glistening in the afternoon sun, he raced out of the car towards the beach with his plastic pail and shovel in his hand.

He spied out some bright, multi-coloured pebbles shining along the shoreline and set about to collect these treasures. One by one, he scooped up each pebble, examined it, and then placed it safely in his little pail. The adults kept a watchful eye on him, chuckling over the amount of energy Steve put into this task.

About ten minutes later, Steve, a normally calm, cool, and collected child, let out a horrifying scream, shocking everyone. Immediately we raced towards him. It was not clear to us what the fuss was all about. Even after we examined him, we could not see a problem. Finally, Steve told us that his eye hurt. Investigating his eye and the area around it, we noticed a small white sore the size of a pinhead, protruding from the bridge of his nose. It resembled a pimple in appearance, and on its own, should not merit any concern.

We dismissed the incident as nothing too serious and tried to distract Steve with more beach fun. Try as we might, Steve still insisted he was in pain. We examined him again, but still no problem was evident. Steve continued to be agitated, insisting he was in pain.

After a while, we decided to take Steve to the local hospital. The doctor on duty carefully examined Steve, taking a close look at the small pimple-like injury on the bridge of his nose. He concluded there was no problem to concern us, other than the fact that Steve had a very low-grade fever. He suggested we give him aspirin to control it. If the "sore" didn't disappear in a day or two, he suggested we then take Steve to our family doctor.

We returned to the cottage around 10 p.m. and tried to put Steve to bed. He just would not settle down. He kept insisting that his eye hurt. After giving him the suggested dose of aspirin, I cradled him in my arms and told him stories until he fell asleep. I turned out the light, walked away and left him to sleep, but often throughout the night, I tiptoed into the room to check on him. I placed my hand on his forehead to check for an increased fever, but I left the light off not to disturb him. His fever remained low grade and Steve slept peacefully until morning.

At the crack of dawn, I went into Steve's room to check on him again. As I entered his room, I almost screamed with shock. What I could not see in the dark as I tiptoed into his room, I could see in the light of day. The right side of Steve's face had grown massive. His right eye, now the size of a golf ball, protruded out in front of an enlarged, deformed face. Immediately I picked him up, and without hesitation, put him in the car and headed for home to take Steve to our family doctor.

One look at Steve and the doctor ordered hospital admittance to an isolation room. Steve was quarantined with no visitors *and no parents* allowed. By the end of the day, the doctors advised that they could not identify the infection causing the massive swelling, nor could they stop its rapid advancement. Somehow, an unusual infection resistant to antibiotics had entered through the small pimple on the bridge of Steve's nose, and the doctors were powerless to stop it.

They estimated that within five to ten hours, the infection would invade the brain and shortly thereafter, probably by morning, take Steve's life. Since they did not know what they "had on their hands", they would not allow anyone near him, except for nursing staff dressed in sterile gowns. I was sent home to wait. Forbidden near my own child, I had no choice but to leave him to die in the arms of strangers.

These events left me numbed, and so much so that I could not relate Steve's condition to anyone. I told my parents that Steve had been admitted to the hospital and was quarantined. I said I would advise them of any changes. Around 10:00 p.m., my husband came home. He was surprised to find someone home. I was so distressed that I neglected to call him. I then related to him quickly about the incident and concluded with the same information I had given to my parents. I could not bring myself to tell anyone the seriousness of Steve's condition. I was frozen in shock.

Gary ate his supper then went to bed for the evening. I paced the floor for hours. About 1:30 a.m., I lowered my exhausted body onto the living room floor, rested my tear-stained face on the carpet, and somehow drifted off to sleep. An hour or so later, I was awakened by the presence of someone in the room.
At first, I thought my husband, Gary, came to inquire why I was not in bed, but as I became more conscious of the form, I noticed a supernatural stream of love and

compassion flowing towards me. I knew it was YeHoVaH. His Spirit began to speak to me. He told me that I needed to completely release Steve to Him.

It seemed to me at that moment, YeHoVaH placed Steve in my hands. With my hands cupped together as if I were holding Steve, and with tears filling my eyes, I released Steve to YeHoVaH. With a wavering, shaky voice I declared: "Whether Steve lives or dies, he belongs to You, YeHoVaH."

Moments after my prayer, along with an intense crying and weeping, I felt *a groaning arise* from deep within. The groaning increased with intensity. To me this resembled the labour pains I experienced when I gave birth to Steve, but this time, there was no pain, only the groaning.

Amidst my groaning, my thoughts began to reflect on my inexperience in YeHoVaH and my past religious beliefs. I was just a new Christian, not even a year in YeHoVaH. I had never heard of "groaning" as a form of prayer! I had grown up in a family that did not share a born-again faith.

When I married, since I did not know YeHoVaH at that time, I married into a family where no one, not my husband nor in-laws, shared the born-again experience. When YeHoVaH saved me ten years into my marriage, I was the first one saved on both sides of the family. This meant unexplained ground without a point of reference. It was new territory for me to travel on. Often, I was uncomfortable, but trust in YeHoVaH budded as we walked together in this somewhat lonely place. All this time, while I was groaning and reflecting, the Presence of YeHoVaH surrounded me and reassured me of the Holy Spirit's help.

My thoughts came full circle to my new faith, where I had recently learned to cling to the scriptures, especially the passage that promised to save my household. I remembered Steve was not yet born again, so I reminded YeHoVaH of the condition of my young son … unsaved. For some five-year-old children, that might not be a problem, but Steve was past the age of reason. He was a bright little boy, with a very high IQ. He clearly knew right from wrong. I knew he must make a choice for salvation.

Once again, YeHoVaH calmed my fears and agitations. He gently reminded me that He was greater than the situation. I listened to His comforting words and continued to pray in the way He led me. I prayed *in this Weeping and Groaning* manner for quite a while until I felt a deep peace envelope me. At that moment, I felt confident that Steve would be healed. I fell asleep until morning.

As daylight streamed through my living room window, I promptly jumped to my feet, grabbed the phone, and called the hospital. The duty nurse informed me that during the night there had been a marvellous change in Steve. His fever had broken, and the swelling began to go down. She said his improvement was so tremendous that the doctor ordered him to be removed from the isolation room to a place where he could have visitors.

Later, when I went to the hospital, I spoke to the doctor in person. He told me that, prior to going home the night before, he checked on Steve. At that point, the antibiotics had not made a difference. In fact, Steve had grown worse. The doctor fully expected Steve would die before morning. He was totally surprised to find an improvement in Steve by morning, and one so drastic that he could be removed from isolation.

Even though the doctor had no *medical* explanation for the sudden disappearance of Steve's infection, I knew the Great Physician visited Steve during the night and healed him.

This intercession is termed:
"WEEPING AND GROANING INTERCESSION"

To give you a grasp on this type of intercession, I am going to recap the experience and point out some detail's imperative to intercession. I will then align these principles with scripture.

As you read my experience earlier in this chapter, remember I stated that I was in shock, which is a very natural response; however, it meant that I *temporarily denied the situation,* thus explaining why I could not tell my husband or anyone else about the extremity of the circumstances.

Obviously, I was *totally overwhelmed,* and since my walk with YeHoVaH had just begun, *my faith* was not yet at a place where I could understand how to change the circumstances. **This identifies my weaknesses clearly!**

When YeHoVaH asked me to "release" Steve to Him, there came a change of focus. I no longer looked at the situation; but rather I looked at YeHoVaH! In addition, I agreed with YeHoVaH that His will should be done, *even though, at that moment, I didn't know what that will was! I knew He intended to change the situation, but I did not yet understand what that change would look like, or what it would take to initiate that change.*

The Holy Spirit knew however, so He partnered with me to help me pray into YeHoVaH's will, **thus overcoming my weaknesses.** This is very biblical.

Romans 8:26-27
   ²⁶ *Likewise the Spirit also helpeth our infirmities: for we know not what we should pray for as we ought: but the Spirit itself maketh intercession for us with groanings which cannot be uttered.* ²⁷*And he that searcheth the hearts knoweth what is the mind of the Spirit because he maketh intercession for the saints according to the will of God.*

The prayer of "groaning" ebbed from my innermost being <u>as the Holy Spirit prayed through me. An intense crying and weeping also was part of the intercession.</u> I did *not* understand *what* the "groaning" meant, nor did I understand the intense weeping. It was very different than the weeping I did earlier before YeHoVaH came into the situation. The first weeping I did was for me, a natural grieving, but when YeHoVaH initiated the "groaning and weeping", it took on a different focus. The result was a prayer uttered by the Holy Spirit through my vocal cords and aimed directly in the center of YeHoVaH's will. ***This is partnering with the Holy Spirit.*** This partnering assured the expression of the need, ***and released or birthed,*** the answers!

The peace that enveloped me, and the confidence that Steve would be healed, was the assurance to me that the intercession was complete. The result: Steve was visited in the night and healed because YeHoVaH's Power was released into the situation through the powerful use of intercession. I will always be grateful to YeHoVaH for returning our only child to us and ecstatically praise Him for His Intervention in this situation.

His compassion to my broken heart, His understanding of my inexperience with Christianity and my inexperience to the scriptures astounded me. I am equally appreciative of the principles of intercession that He taught me that night. Shortly thereafter, I discovered passages in the Word of YeHoVaH that explained things clearly.

What a powerful form of intercession I learned that night!

What a miracle YeHoVaH released through intercession that changed the situation.

> ### The Agony of Intercession
> *A situation desperate for change!*
> ### The Ecstasy of Intercession
> *Intervention birthing a miracle!*

INTERCESSION'S BASIC COMPONENTS:
There are certain components common to every intercession. Each intercession will have:

A Person: These are the **"who"** of intercession, those performing the intercession. In this chapter, I was the intercessor partnering with the Holy Spirit, thus defining the *"who"* of the intercession in the Agony and Ecstasy of Intercession: The Holy Spirit and me.

A Purpose: All intercession transpires for a reason, or purpose. The purpose is *generally* to build a bridge from the problem to the solution. It is needed to bring answers from heaven to earth to solve the problem. Bridges that intercession build explain the **"why"** of the intercession. In recapping the story in the chapter of Agony and Ecstasy, the bridge reached from the problem, "Steve's sickness", to the Solution, "YeHoVaH's miraculous, healing power".

A Process: This explains **"how"** the intercession transpired, or the method used to build the bridge. The how varies in every intercession since it depends upon the "type or method" of intercession used. In the Agony and Ecstasy, the type used was: "Groaning and Weeping Intercession".

On the next page is a chart summarizing the above information:

INTERCESSION'S BASIC COMPONENTS SUMMARIZED

The Who's involved in intercession (person) The Holy Spirit & the intercessor are Partners in Intercession
The Why is intercession necessary? (purpose) Intercession builds a bridge between **the situation** *(the problem) and* **the solution** *(YeHoVaH)*
The How of *this* intercession done? (process) In this case, intercession was completed through "Groaning & Weeping Intercession".

Various types of intercession are comprised of a mixture of intercessory principles used throughout the time of intercession. The principles of Intercession used in every intercession will vary since their use depends on what YeHoVaH desires.

Understanding the principles of intercession, however, will help one to be open to YeHoVaH's leading, expressing the type of intercession needed for a particular situation.

Now, let's look at what *principles of intercession* were used in the Agony & Ecstasy of Intercession.

PART B

⸻ ⠀⠀)(⠀⠀ ⸻

PRINCIPLES OF INTERCESSION

PRINCIPLE # 1

YeHoVaH Initiated the Intercession

As we have already shown in the passage in Romans, "intercession" is a direct work of the Holy Spirit. At this point, I would like to look at *how* intercession begins. In "Agony and Ecstasy of Intercession", it began because YeHoVaH initiated it. Throughout the Bible, YeHoVaH has often initiated encounters with humankind for the purposes of intercession. Look at the following two examples in the Word, when YeHoVaH initiated an intercession. (*We will look at these two scriptures in more detail later, but for now notice* **"who" initiated** *the intercession*).

Genesis 18:16-32
> *"16 ¶ And the men rose up from thence, and looked toward Sodom: and Abraham went with them to bring them on the way. 17 And the LORD said, Shall I hide from Abraham that thing which I do; 18 Seeing that Abraham shall surely become a great and mighty nation, and all the nations of the earth shall be blessed in him? 19 For I know him, that he will command his*

children and his household after him, and they shall keep the way of the LORD, to do justice and judgment; that the LORD may bring upon Abraham that which he hath spoken of him. 20 And the LORD said, Because the cry of Sodom and Gomorrah is great, and because their sin is very grievous; 21 I will go down now, and see whether they have done altogether according to the cry of it, which is come unto me; and if not, I will know. 22 And the men turned their faces from thence, and went toward Sodom: but Abraham stood yet before the LORD."

"23 ¶ And Abraham drew near, and said, Wilt thou also destroy the righteous with the wicked? 24 Peradventure there be fifty righteous within the city: wilt thou also destroy and not spare the place for the fifty righteous that [are] therein? 25 That be far from thee to do after this manner, to slay the righteous with the wicked: and that the righteous should be as the wicked, that be far from thee: Shall not the Judge of all the earth do right? 26 And the LORD said, If I find in Sodom fifty righteous within the city, then I will spare all the place for their sakes. 27 And Abraham answered and said, Behold now, I have taken upon me to speak unto the Lord, which [am but] dust and ashes: 28 Peradventure there shall lack five of the fifty righteous: wilt thou destroy all the city for [lack of] five? And he said, If I find there forty and five, I will not destroy [it].

29 And he spake unto him yet again, and said, Peradventure there shall be forty found there. And he said, I will not do [it] for forty's sake. 30 And he said [unto him], Oh let not the Lord be angry, and I will speak: Peradventure there shall thirty be found there. And he said, I will not do [it] if I find thirty there. 31 And he said, Behold now, I have taken upon me to speak unto the Lord: Peradventure there shall be twenty found there. And he said, I will not destroy [it] for twenty's sake. 32 And he said, Oh let not the Lord be angry, and I will speak yet but this once: Peradventure ten shall be found there. And he said, I will not destroy [it] for ten's sake."

Sodom and Gomorrah were to be destroyed for their iniquity. As YeHoVaH revealed the circumstances to Abraham, He knew how Abraham would respond. Abraham did not disappoint YeHoVaH, but he used this opportunity to intercede on behalf of the city.

In Exodus 32:9-14

⁹And YeHoVaH said unto Moses, I have seen this people, and, behold, it is a stiffnecked people: ¹⁰Now therefore let me alone, that my wrath may wax hot against them, and that I may consume them: and I will make of thee a great nation. ¹¹And Moses besought YeHoVaH his God, and said, YeHoVaH, why doth thy wrath wax hot against thy people, which thou hast brought forth out of the land of Egypt with great power, and with a mighty hand? ¹²Wherefore

> should the Egyptians speak, and say, For mischief did he bring them out, to slay them in the mountains, and to consume them from the face of the earth? Turn from thy fierce wrath, and repent of this evil against thy people. ¹³Remember Abraham, Isaac, and Israel, thy servants, to whom thou swarest by thine own self, and saidst unto them, I will multiply your seed as the stars of heaven, and all this land that I have spoken of will I give unto your seed, and they shall inherit it forever. ¹⁴And YeHoVaH repented of the evil which he thought to do unto his people.

Here we see YeHoVaH "hot" with anger against the children of Israel, thoroughly disappointed in their lack of response to His constant care. He told Moses that He would consume them and make him a great nation in their place. Moses interceded so the children of Israel would be spared. His line of defence was YeHoVaH's reputation.

In both passages, we see an active relationship with YeHoVaH and His intercessors. In Genesis, we see that YeHoVaH will not keep secrets from His Friend: *(Verse 17)* "*Shall I hide from Abraham that thing which I do*". Intercession was a natural response that flowed out of that friendship. In Exodus you can catch a glimpse of an intimate relationship between YeHoVaH and Moses. YeHoVaH shares His anger and His reasons for that anger, with Moses. Moses appealed to YeHoVaH on the grounds of YeHoVaH's integrity.

This kind of a relationship with YeHoVaH does not spring forth overnight. It comes by continuous encounters with YeHoVaH where His Person is revealed. With both Moses and Abraham, a covenant relationship existed with the Almighty. The same is true with a believer.

When a believer enters a born-again relationship with YeHoVaH, the door to a relationship with YeHoVaH is opened wide. That relationship is grounds for YeHoVaH to initiate intercession. In fact, the expression of intercession is so dear to Him, so important, that He will search for an intercessor.

Ezekiel 22: 30
And I sought for a man among them, that should make up the hedge, and stand in the gap before me for the land, that I should not destroy it: but I found none.

Isaiah 59: 16
And he saw that there was no man, and wondered that there was no intercessor:

These two passages clearly indicate YeHoVaH's zeal to find intercessors. When found, He initiates the intercession. The question remains, then, when YeHoVaH looks for an intercessor, will you?

WHO INITIATES AN INTERCESSION?

True intercession proceeds from the heart of YeHoVaH and searches for fulfillment. As a believer, we are the main component for that fulfillment. An invitation is extended towards us to intercede, either by a *direct encounter* initiated by YeHoVaH, or by an *indirect encounter*.

In a direct encounter, we know YeHoVaH has initiated the intercession, but in an indirect encounter, it is less obvious, since the intercession manifests through a desire within the believer. Some interpret this to mean the believer initiates the intercession.

While I can understand that thinking, I hold to another thought. Yeshua said: *(Luke 18:19) Why callest thou me good? None is good, save one, that is, God.* A desire for intercession is a profoundly good desire, but can it spring forth from a person by virtue of his or her own goodness? Personally, I don't think so. The way I understand the workings of YeHoVaH, is that first, He implants the desire and then the believer responds to it, thus engaging in intercession. In other words, YeHoVaH extends an invitation for intercession, but His covenant partner must respond.

At this point, I would like to look at what happens *after* the desire to intercede is recognized and expressed. To act upon desire is to step forward inside the door to intercession, but the intercession has yet to take place. For intercession to transpire, the Holy Spirit must join with the believer, ordaining all that is necessary to fulfill the intercession. An intercessor's zeal, initiatives and wisdom are not sufficient to complete the intercession.

Human qualities cannot generate good intercession, however, *regenerated* human qualities, renewed through a union with YeHoVaH, can form the foundation so that YeHoVaH initiated intercession will transpire. Good intercession is effective intercession. Effective intercession recognizes the believer's inabilities and total dependence upon YeHoVaH, and it acknowledges a sincere and desperate need to connect with YeHoVaH.

Effective intercession has no direction of its own, but rather seeks the direction of YeHoVaH. It also has no selfish desires, but rather empties of self to embrace YeHoVaH's desires. Effective intercession yearns for YeHoVaH and His input at every point.

In conclusion, believers cannot initiate intercession through their *own abilities. Only as believers' partner with* YeHoVaH *can intercession take place.* Intercession is the privilege of a covenant relationship with YeHoVaH, where YeHoVaH presents the intercession and the believer, His covenant partner, responds.

PRINCIPLE # 2
Wait on YeHoVaH for His leading and guidance

Waiting on YeHoVaH for His Leading and Guidance may seem an obvious thing but strangely enough, it is often overlooked. Humankind can be very determined! Our own mindsets can get us in trouble. ***Holy Spirit centered intercession will house only the mindset of the Spirit.*** *Before* proceeding in intercession, at regular points *during* intercession, and when we think the intercession is almost *finished*, we should check with the Holy Spirit to see if we are fully aligned with Him.

At every point, it is imperative we follow YeHoVaH's leading, and *not establish our own path*. The believer's part is to be open to His leading and thus to do things His Way so that YeHoVaH's plans, and purposes are fulfilled, and the intercession does not run ahead of Him, nor come behind. If we follow closely, we'll stay connected with Him.

In my life, I have learned to follow the anointing and the promptings of the Holy Spirit. When the anointing increases in intensity, the intercession does as well, but when the anointing lifts, I take a moment to wait and ask YeHoVaH "why" this has happened. At times, the anointing lifted because I missed a direction change. Without realizing it, I shifted away from the established pattern YeHoVaH set for *this intercession.*

At other times, the anointing lifted because YeHoVaH placed a "pause" in the intercession. The pause was for various reasons: perhaps someone in my household needed attention; perhaps I was tired and needed a break; or perhaps the remainder of the day, for whatever reason, did not lend itself any further to intercession.

I have found that YeHoVaH knows when to initiate the intercession, when to give a break, and when to re-engage and finish as well. Everything eventually becomes evident as the intercession progresses. A key to stay in tune with the Spirit is to closely monitor the anointing. A good rule of thumb is this:

- When the anointing increases in intensity, *flow with it*
- When the anointing decreases ... *pause and inquire.*
- When the anointing lifts or ceases ... *Stop. Inquire. Wait.*

This close "ear" to YeHoVaH will bring good results with a fulfillment of YeHoVaH's will in the intercession and the situation. This principle of waiting on YeHoVaH is important when you pray alone, but it amplifies in importance when you pray in a group. Strong personalities, without realizing it, can pull an entire group in a direction other than what YeHoVaH had planned. This happens because someone is not in agreement with the direction of the intercession. Sometimes one person might believe YeHoVaH for one result, while another believes YeHoVaH for a different result.

It is also possible that doubt may be in the room. This can lead to a "safe" group direction where no one steps out in faith, thus missing the "challenge", or the "walking on water" experience that YeHoVaH wants the group to experience. The direction the group is pulled may seem right because of *the pull of the majority*, but if that direction is aligned with the mindset of the Lord, it might be discovered that it missed His mark. **It is extremely important to listen to the anointed leader and to follow the leading of the Holy Spirit.**

The key to an intercessor's success, whether alone, in a group, or leading a group, is to be mindful of YeHoVaH, His Presence and His will, listening for His Directives at every bend in the road. It is to engage in YeHoVaH's business of the kingdom, under His leadership. This follows closely with what Yeshua taught when He said: **"Thy kingdom come.**

Thy will be done in earth, as *it is* in heaven." Intercessors must wait for His Guidance, His Wisdom, and His Insights. Wait whenever there is a lull in the intercession or an indication of a change of direction.

PRINCIPLE # 3

The Holy Spirit partnered with the believer

This principle, like the first two, may seem obvious as well, but to overlook it would be disastrous. It is important to remember you have a partner in intercession. Intercession is about relationship. First, you know the Person YeHoVaH and then His Power is made available to you. The knowledge that your Heavenly Partner teams with you will bring comfort when you move in intercession. You will know the Greater One is with you, and for you.

It will eliminate any independent spirit you might develop. There is a covenant relationship in Christianity. Covenant relationship implies "Partners" who agree with one another. YeHoVaH designed every aspect of our relationship with Him to include partnering with Him, and intercession is no different:

1. **You cannot be saved alone, without Messiah!** YeHoVaH made a covenant of salvation for all who will receive it. It is our choice whether we receive it. Salvation has two partners: YeHoVaH and you!

2. ***You cannot live out your faith alone, without Messiah!*** The initial faith to believe YeHoVaH for salvation is a gift.[7] To continue serving Him, scripture teaches us: *"The just shall live by faith".* [8]Operating in any of the Gifts of the Spirit requires active faith. Two very active partners at work here: 1) YeHoVaH (via His Gift of faith, His Word, etc.) and 2) you!

3. ***You cannot have revelation of YeHoVaH, without His Help!*** To understand YeHoVaH the Holy Spirit reveals Him to you. The Holy Spirit uses the Word, and at times, Divine Encounters, but it still takes two: *The Holy Ghost to reveal and your willingness to receive.*

4. ***You cannot intercede (or pray) alone!*** The scriptures house the revealed will of YeHoVaH, *but* these are spiritually discerned. Without the help of the Holy Spirit, you will not fully understand the Word. When situations arise and you feel His Will is undefined, uncertain in your thinking, the Holy Spirit may present you with a Rhema Word or another revelation from YeHoVaH to help you understand YeHoVaH's will. All of this requires

---

[7] *Ephesians 2:8 For by grace are ye saved through faith; and that not of yourselves: it is the gift of God*

[8] *Romans 1:17 For therein is the righteousness of God revealed from faith to faith: as it is written, The just shall live by faith.*

the help of YeHoVaH. Two partners again! The believer and YeHoVaH.

YeHoVaH designed our life on earth to include Him. The sooner we realize that and partner with Him, the more effective our Christian life will be.

As far as intercession goes, *please remember, YeHoVaH desires to partner with you!* He will always be the "Senior Partner" so to speak, and ***you will always be the "apprentice"***. In intercession, as with other areas of our lives where we partner with YeHoVaH, the miraculous can happen by *virtue of that partnership*!

It is my firm belief that YeHoVaH extends "a call of intercession" to every covenant partner, or every believer. Some answer those calls and learn its depths, enabled by the Holy Spirit to move heaven and earth with intercession. Others sit on the peripheral edge, uncertain of the waters, and not sure how to safely enter in, and others consider the task not for them, and ignore it altogether.

This scenario seems much like the ins and outs of Christianity, as I see it. Some believers swim in the pool of the Holy Ghost and spend their lives trying to exhaust every avenue of the Christian experience, while others tiptoe around the edges of Christianity looking for fulfillment, not knowing what direction to take[9].

---

[9] This is an observation, for which prayer arises, not a criticism.

Let me encourage you to jump into intercession! Learn its depths! You will find it a most exciting life! No matter how much you learn, there will always be more to learn! You will find intercession a wonderful opportunity to grasp and the rewards astounding.

PRINCIPLE # 4

The focus was shifted from the situation to YeHoVaH & His ability

In the First Covenant, as you read it, you can easily see the Hand of YeHoVaH performing great miracles for the children of Israel while they were in Egypt, during their exodus, and throughout their journey to Canaan Land. Unfortunately, whenever they experienced miracles, they did not fix them in their minds as signatures of YeHoVaH's ability.

When they arrived in Canaan land and saw the giants in the land, since their memories were not marked with the wonders of YeHoVaH, they could not believe YeHoVaH for the task of taking Canaan Land. Instead, they looked at their own ability and saw themselves as grasshoppers. In short, the Israelites (except for Joshua and Caleb) *saw the problem, not the solution*!

If the believer's focus **remains** on the unattainable **circumstances**, believers will **never see beyond** the impossible characteristics. If, on the other hand, the focus of the believer is on YeHoVaH and His ability, then impossible circumstances will be seen as conquerable. The "giant", whatever face it wears, will be tread under our feet like a grasshopper, because our vision was not impaired by "impossibilities", but was rather enhanced by our knowledge and faith in YeHoVaH's abilities.

To rise above difficult situations, to be "lifted" to a place beyond the problem, we need a catalyst called faith. Thinking about YeHoVaH's power and capabilities will cause faith to bubble in your soul and understanding His character *and His desire to help you, will give you confidence that He will respond to your petitions.*

Thinking on these things will build your faith and employ the catalyst you need. Just remember*: the resolution of the situation is not yours to perform; it is your partner's!* Focus on Him and you will see awesome results!

PRINCIPLE # 5
Agreement with YeHoVaH

This is a very basic principle of the Christian faith. The first time a believer uses this principle of agreement is at salvation, when they agree with YeHoVaH and admit they are sinners. The next step in the salvation process is receiving Yeshua as Saviour. At that point, the principle of agreement is used again, and finally, to walk out the Christian life, agreement with YeHoVaH comes in a total surrender to accept YeHoVaH's plan of living out the saved life. In other words, *a lifetime commitment to YeHoVaH triggers a lifetime agreement with YeHoVaH.*

In intercession, our first agreement with YeHoVaH is to align with Him in the act of intercession itself. As we proceed in the intercession, we enter into a continuous agreement with Him when we deem Him to be greater than the situation *(as we saw in the point above)*, and when we trust Him to release His Abilities into a situation to overrule, overcome, or conquer the problem.

Our agreement with YeHoVaH is *active* agreement, not a *hope* that His hand will move. Our agreement with YeHoVaH **_believes_** and releases *"faith"* into the situation, trusting that His Hand *will move*. Agreement with YeHoVaH is much easier when we have a plain revelation of His will in the matter, *but* we don't always have that luxury.

Without clear direction, we agree by *blind faith* to His will, knowing it is the best thing for the situation; so, whether we have a clear line on His will, to bring us into agreement with Him, we can boldly and confidently declare into any situation: "Thy Will be done!" *It's that simple to come into agreement with His Will!*

While an intercession can benefit by an agreement to YeHoVaH's will, the intercessor also has a lesson here. Learning to trust by "blind faith" is training ground for "blind intercession". *"Blind intercession" is a term given to intercession that arises in your spirit without the specifics of the situation being mentally understood.*

In other words, you don't have a clue what's going on! All you know is that you are in intercession. As the intercession unfolds, facts are usually revealed and the YeHoVaH's will with it. This may come by a word of knowledge, a vision, or information revealed another way. No matter when a mental grasp of the intercession is attained, the important thing is to enter into agreement with YeHoVaH and stay in that agreement.

To understand this principle, keep this in mind: to agree with YeHoVaH is to ensure His Will is implemented throughout the intercession, and inevitably, into the situation also. To build your confidence in any intercession where you do not have a mental understanding of all the facts, remember, YeHoVaH is your Senior Partner, and as such, He is the only One with all the facts about the intercession and the situation necessitating it, and He is orchestrating the entire business.

YeHoVaH' always has a purpose for either exposing or temporarily concealing the depths of an intercession. If we find ourselves in the concealed aspect of intercession, we move into "blind intercession".

Operating in such produces good results as we trust in the Holy Spirit. In the end, whether you have a mental understanding or not, the truth is, intercessor only know part of the whole, anyway. They know as much as God sees fit to release.

This fact holds true when praying for cities, regions, and nations, too. For example, one intercessor focuses on one part of the problem; another intercessor will focus on another part; and still others focus on yet another part. It has been my experience that not one intercessor has all the facts and called to pray out all the intercessions.

Remembering that should keep you from feeling "incompetent" when you cannot *mentally* grasp the total intercession. Really, there is no need for us to know all the facts. Furthermore, there is no need for us to draw conclusions about people, circumstances, or places with the facts we know.

Drawing conclusions from our times of intercession is never a good idea, anyway. It is like trying to solve a puzzle with puzzle pieces missing. That just doesn't work! Remember, as an intercessor, faithfully do you part and allow YeHoVaH to reveal whatever He needs to do to get the job done. After all, He is the One directing it all because He is the One Who understands it all! Amen?

PART C

PRINCIPLES OF INTERCESSION CONT'D

PRINCIPLE # 6

YeHoVaH's promises from the Word used as reminders to see them fulfilled.

One devoted intercessor was quoted as saying: "Intercession is **empty** without the Word of YeHoVaH". This is good advice!

As you explore that statement, you will find it holds a double meaning about the "Word" of YeHoVaH! It has its obvious meaning, namely that the "Bible" should be quoted, but it also has another meaning.

The "Word" is another name for Yeshua! Without the person of "The Word" (Yeshua), intercession is empty. Also, remember, the Holy Spirit is the Spirit of Yeshua! Therefore, in intercession we need the following components:

- The Person, the Word, the Holy Spirit
- The Rhema Word (Alive Word, quickened by the Holy Spirit to give direction to the intercession)
- The Revealed Word (the Bible)

When we desire YeHoVaH to move on our behalf or that of another, we simply remind Him of His Word. YeHoVaH has bound Himself to respond to His Word *as He has declared it.* As we present His Word to Him, we do not demand that He fulfill His Commitments to us. We present Yeshua's Word with an attitude of thanksgiving for it, thinking of it as a Gift. In your heart, you know His Integrity to His Word will ensure that it is fully realized. He will not fail to keep His Word to you!

In intercession with my son, (Agony and Ecstasy of Intercession) I didn't know much scripture, but I did know that YeHoVaH *promised my entire household will be saved!* This was the promise of YeHoVaH that I held before Him because Steve was not saved. Granted, he was only five years old, but mentally he was older. In fact, when he was tested in school at 7 years of age, they discovered he had the understanding and reasoning capacity of a 16-year-old. At 5, he clearly knew right from wrong and could make choices.

The Word I presented to YeHoVaH was Acts 26:31: *³¹And they said, Believe on the Lord Jesus Christ, and thou shalt be saved, and thy house.* The faithfulness of YeHoVaH to *His Promise of Household Salvation* was (and still is) so intense, if He must raise someone from the dead to keep His Word, He will ... *especially if one of His Children is holding on to His Promise!*

In intercession, we cannot underestimate the value of the Word of YeHoVaH. Extend His Promised Word. Watch YeHoVaH perform what He has promised. He will never fail, nor disregard His promises. In fact, He will even encourage you to present the promises to Him, since they were given for that purpose.

PRINCIPLE # 7
Wait on YeHoVaH for His Leading & Guidance

Earlier, we classified the "Agony and Ecstasy of Intercession" as a type of intercession. Here we will define it as a principle of intercession since it can be both a principle and a type of intercession. We will explain this in more detail later. For now, we'll look at it as a principle of intercession.

HOW DOES THE HOLY SPIRIT HELP US?
First, please re-read *Romans 8: 26- 27.*[10] Then read on.

- The Holy Spirit helps us by making intercession with *groans* that cannot be understood, or in other words, with *sounds that are "unspeakable"*
- These sounds seem unintelligible to us
- These sounds are understood by YeHoVaH and responded to as well

---

[10] *Romans 8:26-27*
Likewise, the Spirit also helps our infirmities: for we know not what is the mind of the Spirit, because he maketh intercession for us with groanings which cannot be uttered. And he that searcheth the hearts knoweth what is the mind of the Spirit because he maketh intercession for the saints according to the will of YeHoVaH.

Often an intercession may *begin* with groaning. It arises *first* in the believer's spirit and when expressed, it often looks or sounds like a pregnant woman in labour. The groaning may go on for a moment or two, or a prolonged period. This may be all that the intercession entails, or it is also possible that "groaning" will *not* even become part of an intercession.

When groaning is included as part of the intercession, it may transpire for a time, and cease for a time, while other principles of intercession are used, and then return at a later point in the intercession. Frequently, if an intercession is "stalled" for any reason, and/or the intercessor doesn't know how to proceed, it is very possible the groaning will start again.

There are no hard and fast rules

on any principles of intercession.

They are used as the Holy Spirit wills.

Any principles used in intercession
will always be the choice of YeHoVaH.

After over twenty years of intercessory experience with YeHoVaH, I can tell you: *no two intercessory experiences* have ever been alike! There have been similarities, using principles common in other intercessions, but the order of use may differ, the length of time each one is employed may also vary. Every intercession, in my experience, has been unique.

PRINCIPLE # 8

Intercession was made to YeHoVaH through weeping

Weeping intercession can be found in Hebrews 5:7 *(Yeshua) Who in the days of his flesh, when he had offered up prayers and supplications with* **<u>strong crying and tears</u>** *unto him that was able to save him from death.* A look at the Greek words for "<u>strong crying and tears</u>" reveals something interesting:

    5. The Greek word here, translated in the King James Version as "<u>*strong*</u>*,*" can also mean **boisterous**. This is not gentle crying! This is crying that is loud.

6. The Greek word translated as *"crying"* can also mean an *outcry* and can carry connotations of *great grief or turmoil, expressed very loud, with clamour.* *Synonyms for clamour include scream, screech, and bellow.* (Not too quiet is it!)
7. The Word interpreted as *"tears"* is straightforward and is the same, as we know it today.

Scripture illustrates Yeshua interceding with loud and boisterous **cries** showing His great grief or turmoil. Quite a picture isn't it! It is not at all the way some artists have painted Him. Let's put the artist's picture out of our mind and hold to the picture painted by the Word. Realize too, if Yeshua prayed in such an intense manner, His followers, who are like Him, may do so also.

PRINCIPLE # 9

Intercession transpired until a peace came

Philippians 4: 6

> [6] *Be careful for nothing; but in every thing by prayer and supplication with thanksgiving let your requests be made known unto God.* [7] *And the peace of God, which passeth all understanding, shall keep your hearts and minds through Christ Jesus*

To reiterate this scripture, when troubled by a situation, bring it to YeHoVaH. When the request is made known to YeHoVaH, and is fully prayed out, you will enjoy a peace that surpasses all understanding.

As you walk through an intercession, you "carry" the burden to YeHoVaH until it is lifted, or in other words, until the intercession is completed, and you have received a peace that surpasses all understanding. This process of carrying the intercession is called, "an assignment." Your assignment has a beginning, steps, or stages to fulfill within, and an end. The assignment, especially a short one, may be done all at once.

Longer assignments, or assignments that expend a lot of energy, may have various stages, with periods of rest in between and may take much longer to fulfill. Some assignments transpire over days, weeks, or months, etc. with rest periods in between. Some intercession requires a natural exploration of facts, especially when interceding for regions, cities, and nations. YeHoVaH, therefore, places the time for that research or investigation within the stages of the intercession.

Remember, the entire timeframe and contents of the intercession are in His Hands. He knows the intercessor and their life, the requirements on the intercessor's time, the time sequences of the intercession, and all the other details. The intercessor only needs to follow YeHoVaH, one step at a time.

The total number of steps *may* be revealed ahead of time, especially if the assignment is a short one, but if it is not, the steps may be revealed only as they are approached. An intercessor intercedes when called to do so, and then, when the assignment shifts to a rest, the intercessor rests.

Stages of intercession have a purpose, just like the stages of a pregnant woman in labour. A release will follow each stage, along with an assurance the assignment is finished. *(This is explained in the next point.)* When the total assignment has been completed, peace will resonate from your spirit.

Whenever you think about the intercession, there will be a sense of completion. You know there is nothing left to do!

PRINCIPLE # 10

Assurance was given by YeHoVaH

that the intercession was complete

A deep peace comes when an intercession is complete, but the assurance goes one step further. If a miracle is needed, YeHoVaH implants, in your spirit, the knowledge that the miracle is on its way.

You might not see any evidence in the natural. In fact, the evidence may seem to the contrary, but you are certain, assured by the Holy Spirit, that the intercession is complete. This assurance enables you to rest or settle back into the peace YeHoVaH gave you, fully convinced that He has heard you and is bringing the miracle to its point of manifestation.

> 1 John 5:14-15
>
> [14]*And this is the confidence* (also translated assurance) *that we have in him, that, if we ask any thing according to his will, he heareth us:* [15]*And if we know that he hear us, whatsoever we ask, we know that we have the petitions that we desired of him.*

Once this confidence or assurance has filled your spirit, hang on to it. If negative thoughts rise, remove them with the Word. Remind yourself of His Promises. If you think you ended your intercession too early, talk to YeHoVaH about it! He will let you know if you have. YeHoVaH *wants* to give you the petitions you asked of Him, since He desires the best for you, and for all involved in any intercession.

You can trust Him to help you in any and every way that He can so that you can obtain what He has promised. He is not "holding things back". No! He is waiting to release them to you! Remember, He is on your side!!!

THIS CHAPTER's CONCLUSION

In this chapter, we analyzed the event that began my intercessory journey with YeHoVaH. Through this event, the components of intercession were pointed out and placed in a chart to show the Who, the Why and the How of the intercession used in "Agony and Ecstasy of Intercession". Although we stated the "how" of intercession was "Weeping & Groaning intercession", we did not give a definition for the intercession.

Let's define Weeping and Groaning Intercession, but first, I would like to remind you of a statement written earlier in the introduction entitled "Before Intercession". There I wrote: "My intentions *(for writing this book)* are not to write an encyclopaedia on the subject, *(intercession)* **nor to put intercession into little theological boxes either.**"

Please keep that comment in mind whenever you read any aspects or definitions about intercession. When intercession is operative, "types" will stretch beyond any defined borders, swing from one type of intercession to another, and often combine several types together. Definitions in intercession cannot be all inclusive with tight borders. We must leave room for overlap.

Now, let's focus on Weeping and Groaning Intercession. Please note "weeping and groaning" are also *principles of intercession.* As principles, (# 7 & 8) each one can be used separately or together within any other type of intercession. As a type of intercession, a definition of such requires that *"Weeping and Groaning"* transpire consistently throughout the intercession. In other words, *this intercession type* frames around the w*eeping and* *groaning principle* active throughout the intercession activity.

When the Holy Spirit draws you into intercession of any kind, I don't expect Him to tell you: *Today we are going to do Weeping and Groaning Intercession.* However, I do expect Him to use the principles in this and other chapters. When in intercession, if a groaning arises in your spirit, respond and yield to it. If you suddenly wish to cry, and cry loudly, express it. Now that you know these principles exist, you can have a confidence that YeHoVaH works in this manner, and then you can obey His promptings and do what He requires of you.

When in intercession, don't worry about understanding what "type" of intercession it is going to be, or think about how many principles the intercession will use. None of that matters!

Remember, these principles and types are only defined for the purposes of teaching and learning. Enjoy your time of intercession with YeHoVaH and keep your mind on Him. After all, intercession is all about your relationship with YeHoVaH. Connect with Him. Fulfill His desires.

Be the vessel of intercession He longs for. In that way, your intercession will be powerful, effective, and most enjoyable to you and YeHoVaH.

DEFINITION:

WEEPING & GROANING INTERCESSION

Weeping and Groaning Intercession is a powerful form of intercession that encompasses an entire intercession. Groans *(unutterable sounds)* and/or weeping *(even as YeHoVaH did with loud cries)* are released **by the Holy Spirit** through the vessel, *(the believer)* directly into the center of YeHoVaH's will, to release His Power into a situation. It is usually operative where human knowledge is inadequate. At times, the intercessor may not know the reason for the "weeping and groaning intercession" and may not understand what fruit it has brought forth either. Nevertheless, since the Holy Spirit births it, eternal results are produced, thus accomplishing what human beings could never have done alone.

LET THINGS SIMMER:

This book will cover a lot of ground about intercession. Quite often, what is explained, the reader has yet to experience. If that is the way it is with you, just let everything simmer in the back of your mind.

As you seek YeHoVaH about intercession and the validity of the material in this book, you will build a far greater relationship with Him than you have already. When He thinks you are ready to experience any type of intercession in this book, He will validate the material and lead you in the direction you can handle. Until that time, rest in the Lord and keep open to intercessory possibilities in your life.

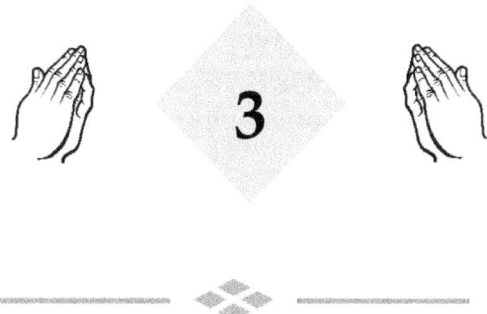

THE SHOCKING REALITY OF VISIONS

Early, one sunny afternoon, my husband and I were driving down the highway to visit some family who lived just a short distance away. Since I was the passenger and not the driver, I decided to take a quick nap. I closed my eyes, but immediately opened them again. *In that split second when my eyes were closed, I had a vision.* This is what I saw: a young teenage boy drowning in a lake. With my eyes wide-open now, the vision continued. I could see the complete situation clearly, as if watching a movie on a television screen.

While swimming in the lake, a young teenage boy had developed a problem. Although he was nearing the shore, the water was still deep, way over his head. When I saw him in the vision, the young man began to sink beneath the surface of the water. As he sank, he swallowed big mouthfuls of water. No one was around to see the teenager was in trouble and help him to safety. Without some help, this young man would surely drown.

As soon as I saw the life-threatening situation, I petitioned the Lord to impart strength to the young man, and I prayed for the angels of YeHoVaH to uphold him. It was clear that the teenager was in a panic, and if something did not happen immediately, he was sure to die. As I petitioned YeHoVaH for help, I saw a floating dock projecting from the shore. It was hard to tell if the teenager, in his panicked state, could even reach the dock, especially when he wasn't looking in that direction. I asked YeHoVaH to calm the young man, show him the dock, and direct him there.

As I prayed, YeHoVaH did just that. The teenager calmed down and began to look around. As he did, he saw the dock and began to move towards it. He reached the dock, crawled on it, and with his face flat against the boards, he passed out. This concerned me since he had swallowed so much water. I asked YeHoVaH to arouse the young man and help him to expel the water he had ingested. Then, the young boy woke up, spit out big mouthfuls of water, and then got up, staggered away from the dock, and headed straight towards a nearby cottage. The vision ended and the intercession with it.

My husband and I continued our way, visited with family, then returned home a little later in the day. Shortly before it was time to leave for Sunday evening church service, a young teenage boy from the church named Jeff came to our home. He told me, with great emotion, that he nearly died that afternoon. This is what he told me.

After church service on Sunday morning, Jeff stayed behind with some other members of the youth group. They had planned to go on a picnic together, but the event was cancelled. Instead, the group decided to go to the pastor's cottage. While at the cottage, early in the afternoon, immediately after lunch, while the other youth group members were playing crochet on the cottage lawn, Jeff decided he'd go for a swim. Without asking for permission, he left the group and went swimming alone in the nearby lake.

The lake was extremely cold, and he was not in it too long before he developed strong stomach cramps. They were severe and strong enough to cause him to double up with the pain. His body became locked in this bent position and Jeff was unable to straighten it out. He began to sink beneath the water. Each time he went below the surface, he came up spitting out big mouthfuls of water. He tried continually to straighten his body, but no matter how hard he tried, he just couldn't do it. He knew he was about to drown.

Terrified, Jeff cried to YeHoVaH to help him. Suddenly his body straightened out. He calmed down and as he did, he saw a floating dock sticking out from the shore. He found the strength to swim to it. Crawling upon the dock, he fell on it face down. He said he lost awareness for a moment. Then something woke him up. He began to spew out the big mouthfuls of water that he had ingested. Jeff then staggered back to the cottage exhausted, and there on the pastor's lawn, in the afternoon sun, he fell asleep.

As I listened to Jeff, I silently praised YeHoVaH for the intercession earlier that day. When Jeff finished relating his story, I re-emphasized the importance of the basic water safety rules that he violated and then, to build his faith in YeHoVaH that answers prayers, I briefly shared the intercession that transpired that afternoon. We both were appreciative of YeHoVaH's intervention that saved him, Jeff of course, more appreciative than I!

Jeff had learned from his foolish choice and gained a new appreciation for rules designed to protect him. This young man went to church that Sunday evening blessing YeHoVaH for hearing his desperate cry and for giving him all that he needed to save him from drowning. My heart was filled with gratitude too, delighted to have been YeHoVaH's intercessory partner to bring a happy ending to an otherwise tragic event.

This intercession is termed:
SITUATIONAL INTERCESSION

In situational intercession, a circumstance *is already in progress*. The intercessor receives pertinent information about the incident, either through natural means or by supernatural means. Intercession then takes place to **bring YeHoVaH's intervention into the situation and change it.**

A biblical example of *situational intercession* is found in the book of Jonah:

> Jonah 2: 1-10:.
> ¹Then Jonah prayed (also translated interceded) unto YeHoVaH his God out of the fish's belly, ²And said, I cried by reason of mine affliction unto YeHoVaH, and he heard me; out of the belly of hell cried I, and thou heardest my voice. ³For thou hadst cast me into the

deep, in the midst of the seas; and the floods compassed me about: all thy billows and thy waves passed over me. ⁴Then I said, I am cast out of thy sight; yet I will look again toward thy holy temple. ⁵The waters compassed me about, even to the soul: the depth closed me round about, the weeds were wrapped about my head. ⁶I went down to the bottoms of the mountains; the earth with her bars was about me for ever: yet hast thou brought up my life from corruption, O YeHoVaH my God.

⁷When my soul fainted within me I remembered YeHoVaH: and my prayer came in unto thee, into thine holy temple. ⁸They that observe lying vanities forsake their own mercy. ⁹But I will sacrifice unto thee with the voice of thanksgiving; I will pay that that I have vowed. Salvation is of YeHoVaH. ¹⁰And YeHoVaH spake unto the fish, and it vomited out Jonah upon the dry land.

Jonah, although running away from YeHoVaH's call on his life, cried out to YeHoVaH to save him. YeHoVaH responded, spoke to the fish, and Jonah was vomited out on dry land. Even though Jonah's intercession was on his own behalf, and it was a direct result of his own situation, (and for that matter, of his own choices), it is still a good example of Situational Intercession.

It clearly demonstrated YeHoVaH's willingness and ability *to change a situation* while it is in progress, even if it meant changing the heart of the prophet caught in the situation. Although YeHoVaH had prepared the great fish and knew the outcome of the situation, Jonah did not. Jonah's prayer, based on a call for divine mercy and intervention, demonstrates a trust in YeHoVaH to deliver him from his desperate circumstances. This is an excellent biblical example of "situational intercession".

Now, that we've shown Situational Intercession is biblical, let's look at Jeff's Story: "The Shocking Reality of Visions" to determine the principles of intercession in it. Some of these principles will be the same as we learned in the last chapter, while others will be new principles to learn.

PRINCIPLES OF INTERCESSION

In this chapter, "The Shocking Reality of Visions" and in each chapter and intercession thereafter, a chart explains the principles, one at a time, as they appeared in the intercession. Principles learned in previous chapters are listed by number. Below the Number is either a Yes or No, showing if the intercession under study used that principle or not. Beneath the number is the principle's description, and beneath that description are some clarifying comments. After recapping each intercession, New Principles of Intercession appear.

EARLIER PRINCIPLES OF INTERCESSION

1.	YeHoVaH initiated the intercession
Yes	*This intercession came via a vision, revealing the problem and activating the intercession.*
2.	**Wait on YeHoVaH for His Leading and Guidance.**
Yes	*As YeHoVaH directed the intercession, He also gave the solution. As the intercessor, I only needed to wait for His leading to understand His planned solution.*
3.	**The Holy Spirit partnered with the believer.**
Yes	*The Holy Spirit gave specific detail in the intercession to show the direction it must go.*
4.	**The focus was shifted from the situation to YeHoVaH & His ability.**
Yes	*The focus shifted from the "situation" of a drowning victim to YeHoVaH who could affect his rescue.*
5.	**Agreement was made with YeHoVaH.**
Yes	*The intercession itself was active agreement with YeHoVaH to save the teenager.*

6.	**YeHoVaH's promises from the Word used as reminders to see them fulfilled**
No/Yes	*Although I did not hold a promise before YeHoVaH, the young man did. He cried out to YeHoVaH to save him and believed YeHoVaH would do so*
7.	**Intercession was made into the direct will of YeHoVaH through groaning.**
No	*This principle was not used here.*
8.	**Intercession was made to YeHoVaH through weeping.**
Yes	This principle was not used here as I was interceding, but according to Jeff he used loud shrieks!
9.	**Intercession transpired until a peace came.**
Yes	*Peace came when the vision ended.*
10.	**Assurance was given by YeHoVaH, that the intercession was complete.**
Yes	*The vision ended with the young man staggering towards the cottage. The assurance came as the vision ended and the intercession was complete.*

We will continue to analyze "The Shocking Reality of Visions", looking for New Principles of Intercession.

NEW PRINCIPLES OF INTERCESSION

PRINCIPLE # 11

YeHoVaH gave a Word of Knowledge

1 Corinthians 12:8
For to one is given by the Spirit the word of wisdom, to another the word of knowledge by the same Spirit;

A word of knowledge *comes* to you! With it, you will know something that you did not know earlier. You don't search for the information, it just arrives! The Holy Spirit *imparts* the knowledge to you. A word of knowledge can come in many ways:

- *Suddenly*, so you simply know the information
- *Verbally*, as YeHoVaH speaks it clearly to your mind
- *As an impression* by the Holy Spirit so you understand
- *In the form of a vision*, showing something revelatory and humanly impossible to know. Visions can be either open or closed.

Check out the quick recap of both types of visions:

OPEN VISIONS: (Daniel, Revelation)
Open visions are like movies. *Your eyes are open, and you watch the vision as it is projected before you.* The vision can be in full colour, or black and white. People, elements of nature and such are often seen and heard. Contents of the vision depend on the purpose of YeHoVaH. You can interact with this vision.

CLOSED VISIONS (Peter in Acts 10).
Closed visions seem *projected into your mind. Your eyes may be opened or closed.* This vision can be in black and white, or in full colour. People, elements of nature and such can also be seen and heard. Again, the contents and purpose depend on YeHoVaH. You can interact with this vision.

In the case of the "Shocking Reality of Visions", the quick, *closed vision* acted like a word of knowledge informing me that a young teenager was drowning. This closed vision activated the intercession, but the open vision continued it. Either vision by itself could have revealed the complete situation and either one could have been prayed into. I have no logical explanation for YeHoVaH's use of two different vision types during this intercession, but I believe YeHoVaH selected that which would bring about the best results considering both the intercessor and the situation.

PRINCIPLE # 12

The vision was prayed into

A believer can interact with a vision. (Read Daniel or Revelation and you will see people spoke to characters in a vision and received a response.) Visions from YeHoVaH *can* be prayed into *(even if it is a vision YeHoVaH has given for your life's goal)*. We can prophetically speak into a vision, and we can pray or intercede about a vision, or during a vision if necessary. It all depends on the purpose YeHoVaH has for the vision.

In a vision about the future, we are privileged to work with YeHoVaH to bring something to pass, or we work with YeHoVaH to see something happen differently. Any vision YeHoVaH presents will have a purpose.

While speaking about Divine Revelation, let me address dreams that reveal tragedies. Should you experience this, consider it *an invitation for intercession*. Don't ignore it! Don't succumb to a helpless feeling either. Call on YeHoVaH to show you what to do. Perhaps, it is an opportunity to make a difference. Remember:

Daniel 2:22
> *22 He revealeth the deep and secret things: he knoweth what is in the darkness, and the light dwelleth with him.*

YeHoVaH reveals secrets and shares His heart with us. YeHoVaH, help us to listen and respond!

PRINCIPLE # 13
YeHoVaH responded to the Distressful Cry

Psalm 18: 5-6
> *⁵The sorrows of hell compassed me about: the snares of death prevented me. ⁶In my distress I called upon YeHoVaH, and cried unto my God: he heard my voice out of his temple, and my cry came before him, even into his ears.*

Jeff had given his life to YeHoVaH earlier in his childhood years, thus Jeff and YeHoVaH were *in covenant* together. Jeff's choices were irresponsible and placed him in a dangerous situation that could have ended his life, but YeHoVaH's perfect will for Jeff was "Life" and not "Death". After Jeff cried out to YeHoVaH to help him, YeHoVaH initiated an intercession to facilitate the rescue of His drowning child. Praise YeHoVaH for His Mercy, Love and Compassion. Amen!

PRINCIPLE # 14

The angels of YeHoVaH were sent into the situation

My prayer for angels to strengthen Jeff was biblical.

Luke 22:41-43
> *41 And he was withdrawn from them about a stone's cast, and kneeled down, and prayed, 42 Saying, Father if thou be willing, remove this cup from me: nevertheless not my will, but thine, be done. 43 And there appeared an angel unto him from heaven, strengthening him.*

Yeshua was given strength by the angels to continue the difficult task that was before Him. While angels can release strength to human beings, they can also intervene to change a situation. In the book of Acts, an angel appeared when Peter was taken captive and death awaited him

Acts 12: 5-11
> *⁵Peter therefore was kept in prison: but prayer was made without ceasing of the church unto God for him. ⁶And when Herod would have brought him forth, the same night Peter was sleeping between two soldiers, bound with two chains: and the keepers before the door kept the prison. ⁷And, behold, the angel of the Lord came upon him, and a light shined in the prison: and he smote Peter on the side, and raised him up,*

saying, Arise up quickly. And his chains fell off from his hands. ⁸And the angel said unto him, Gird thyself, and bind on thy sandals. And so he did. And he saith unto him, Cast thy garment about thee, and follow me. ⁹And he went out, and followed him; and wist not that it was true which was done by the angel; but thought he saw a vision

¹⁰When they were past the first and the second ward, they came unto the iron gate that leadeth unto the city; which opened to them of his own accord: and they went out, and passed on through one street; and forthwith the angel departed from him. ¹¹And when Peter was come to himself, he said, Now I know of a surety, that the Lord hath sent his angel, and hath delivered me out of the hand of Herod, and from all the expectation of the people of the Jews.

The church began to pray. YeHoVaH sent an angel to break off the chains that bound Peter to the prison, and to lead him past the prison gates.

By the way, this is another good example of "situational intercession". This one began with "human knowledge" of a problem. Peter was in danger of losing his life. The Bible does not tell us exactly what the church prayed, so we can't examine the passage for principles of intercession, but we can see two things:

- *Death awaited Peter.* A situation was set in place to end Peter's life. At this point in Peter's life, he still had much work left to do for YeHoVaH. Premature death was certainly the adversary's plans, but not YeHoVaH's. Intercession aligned the situation with YeHoVaH's plans and purposes for Peter. (Remember, the main reason for situational intercession is to change the situation!)

- *Angels were sent into the situation.* In response to the prayers of the church, YeHoVaH sent an angel to remove Peter's chains and lead Peter out of the prison. Whether or not the church specifically requested this we can't say because the Bible doesn't record it, but the point here is that angels are given a specific task to perform and are sent into situations to complete their assignment.

Whenever you send out angels, remember:
- It is to do YeHoVaH's bidding, to accomplish His purposes
- It is in response to YeHoVaH's prompting
- All attention must be focused on YeHoVaH, never on the angels. Just give them their orders as YeHoVaH instructs you to, and then move on

THIS CHAPTER'S CONCLUSION:

In this chapter, "The Shocking Reality of Visions", we classified the intercession as 'Situational Intercession" and then analyzed the principles of intercession that were active to prevent Jeff from drowning. In a moment, I will define Situational Intercession, but first, I must mention that not every Situational Intercession includes a vision. Natural information can and does present opportunities for situational intercession. *(Remember, Peter in prison.)* For some intercessors, natural information will spur on Situational Intercession more often than a vision.

DEFINITION:
SITUATIONAL INTERCESSION

This intercession takes place while a situation is *in progress*. The Holy Spirit directs the intercession with specific intentions to change the situation as it happens. Intercession is made until the situation is re-aligned to the plans and purposes of YeHoVaH. It may or may not bear the marks of YeHoVaH's intervention.

A PLUG FOR SITUATIONAL INTERCESSION

When YeHoVaH, in His passion for intercession, looks for an intercessor, you can see that it is very important that one be found! How many things would be different, if we made ourselves more available and were more attentive to the passions of YeHoVaH, only heaven knows.

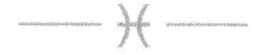

HOW ARE YOU DOING?

Remember, this material is intended to bring you step by step into the depths of intercession and simultaneously, expose you to the possibilities of a greater relationship with YeHoVaH. So, how are you doing? Perhaps, these questions might help you to assess your progress:

1. What have you learned, directly or indirectly, about YeHoVaH?
2. Have you perceived His compassion, His Love, His Desire for you and all humankind to experience his best?
3. How do you feel about drawing closer to YeHoVaH in order to experience, firsthand, what you have learned in this book?

A PRAYER FOR YOU

This prayer comes from the prayer of the Apostle, Paul, found in Ephesians 1:17-23

Heavenly Father: I pray ""**17** That the God of our Lord Jesus Christ, the Father of glory, may give unto you the spirit of wisdom and revelation in the knowledge of him: **18** The eyes of your understanding being enlightened; that ye may know what is the hope of his calling, and what the riches of the glory of his inheritance in the saints, **19** And what *is* the exceeding greatness of his power to us-ward who believe, according to the working of his mighty power, **20** Which he wrought in Christ, when he raised him from the dead, and set *him* at his own right hand in the heavenly *places,* **21** Far above all principality, and power, and might, and dominion, and every name that is named, not only in this world, but also in that which is to come: **22** And hath put all *things* under his feet, and gave him *to be* the head over all *things* to the church, **23** Which is his body, the fulness of him that filleth all in all."

ABOUT JONAH'S INTERCESSION

In this chapter, there is a record of Jonah's situational intercession. Perhaps, you might like to analyze it picking out what principles Jonah used to move the hand of God. Re-read Jonah 2:1-10 and list the principles you find operative. When finished, if you wish to compare it with the author's recap, look for Jonah'

IMPENDING DANGER STRIKES OUT

One winter's night in late February, while relaxing in my favourite chair and snuggled inside a quilted blanket, YeHoVaH led me into another intercession. It began shortly after I listened to the weatherman explain that the worse winter storm in years was about to hit the nation, bringing freezing rain with heavy downfalls of snow in some areas, and fog, followed by torrents of rain, in others. Outside my window, I could hear the storm with its winter wind blowing against the shutters. This noise gave a soundtrack to accompany a vision that began the intercession.

As the vision unfolded, I saw two large transport trucks travelling in the dark of night, along a curvy mountain highway in Western Canada. Patches of ice dotted the highway, and from time to time, blowing snow would sweep across the road reducing visibility to zero. Both trucks drove in the same lane, with one truck following the other, as they climbed higher and higher up the mountain highway.

As the drivers assessed the highway, they could see a deep gorge on their right-hand side, about four feet from the highway's edge. With no room to pull over in an emergency, and with these weather conditions, they knew they must move at slow speeds with great care just to avoid an accident. For safety, both trucks had chains on their tires for greater stability, but still, if either truck hit a patch of ice and lost control of their vehicle, they might slide towards the guardrails, break through them and plummet over the gorge to a terrible death.

As the vision continued, I saw one truck pull into the passing lane to pass the other truck. These two trucks, now travelling almost side-by-side, were only a short distance away from a dangerous bend in the road. Unless they were familiar with the highway, they would not know about that sharp bend. I saw it because YeHoVaH pointed it out to me in the vision. I also saw a third truck, on the other side of the curve, travelling in the lane for oncoming traffic.

Once the three trucks arrived at the bend in the road, a head-on collision in the passing lane would be unavoidable. It was most probable that two truckers would hit head-on. Each trucker would surely die when that happened and the force of their collision would inevitably involve the other truck, in the right-hand lane, ramming truck and trucker through the guardrails and into the deep gorge below.

Knowing the purpose of the intercession was to prevent a terrible accident, I began to intercede that the offending trucker, *(the one making the pass)* would re-assess the situation clearly, realize the danger, and then, pull back into his own lane, behind the truck he was attempting to pass.

Intercession, to this point, did not change the situation, as the trucker continued to attempt his pass. As I asked YeHoVaH for wisdom, the vision zoomed in closer, giving me a better view of the situation. Now I could see details in greater clarity. In the right-hand lane, the trucker about to be passed looked very nervous and agitated by the trucker attempting to pass him.

As I watched this scene, I could feel his desperation as he took his CB in his hand and tried to reach the other trucker. There was no response. He then pulled his air horn several times, but again there was no response as the offending trucker totally ignored him. I continued, to intercede asking YeHoVaH to help the offending trucker change his mind, but the man would not relent. He was going to make that pass if it killed him!

Up to this point in my intercessory experience, immediate changes would always occur as the intercession progressed, but not this time! Something was different and I didn't understand what. I asked YeHoVaH for wisdom. Immediately, rising from my spirit came an authority and from out of my mouth came a command, with a clear directive aimed at the powers of darkness, to *"break the powers"* that fuelled the dangerous situation.[11]

Within moments, the truck in the passing lane began to slow down and pull back in, and might I add, just in time. Trucks do not manoeuvre as quickly as cars, and if he had delayed another few minutes, the inevitable would have taken place, with these three trucks colliding. The trucker in front was relieved when the other trucker pulled behind him, but he was shaking from the trauma. Intercession was made to bring him peace. Then the vision ended.

This intercession occurred on a Monday evening. Fourteen days later, my husband Gary, a long-haul trucker, came home from a road trip. He told me that

---

[11] *Ephesians 6:12 For we wrestle not against flesh and blood, but against principalities, against powers, against the rulers of the darkness of this world, against spiritual wickedness in high places.*

he never expected to see me again. He related this story.

He had been on a run in the sunny southern states when he received orders to drive to Western Canada. A winter blizzard awaited him in Canada, so he wasn't too thrilled about the run. Nevertheless, he accepted the run and headed for Canada. On the Friday evening, a week earlier, in the most wretched weather and road conditions, and at the worse possible spot on a two-lane mountain highway, a truck decided to pass him.

Gary knew there was a tight curve just ahead and, in winter road conditions such as these, a heavy truck would not be able to pass him before the curve. Gary couldn't pull over since the highway did not provide space for that. He slowed down to make it easier for the other trucker to pass him, but the trucker continued to run parallel to him, determined to keep by his side.

Gary thought to himself; "If this guy continues to run beside me when we hit the curve, if there's another truck in the oncoming lane, we'll all be dead." In Gary's mind, he calculated that with the driving conditions, the terrain of the road and the force of the impact when the other two trucks hit, he would take a blow on the left-hand side of his truck. That blow would act like a big hand and sweep him over the cliff. If that happened, he knew he would die. In desperation, he used his CB to warn the other trucker of the bend in the highway, but the trucker would not answer. He pulled his air horn. No response.

Gary was convinced that he was about to die. At that point, he asked YeHoVaH to help him. Immediately after his prayer, the offending trucker pulled in behind him. A few minutes later as Gary approached the curve, he saw what he dreaded: a truck in the lane for oncoming traffic. Gary knew for sure the trucker in the passing lane *did not see* the other truck coming because visibility was too poor for that.

For sure: the hand of YeHoVaH *intervened and saved him from a terrible death.* At that point, I shared about the intercession that had taken place earlier the week before. Together we rejoiced over YeHoVaH's goodness. How gracious and how awesome is YeHoVaH!

Psalm 9: 1-4
> [1] *I will praise thee, O YeHoVaH, with my whole heart; I will shew forth all thy marvellous works.* [2]*I will be glad and rejoice in thee: I will sing praise to thy name, O thou most High.* [3]*When mine enemies are turned back, they shall fall and perish at thy presence.* [4]*For thou hast maintained my right and my cause; thou satest in the throne judging right.*

This intercession is termed:
PREVENTATIVE INTERCESSION

You might look at the similarities between the intercession in "The Shocking Reality of Visions" and this one, "Impending Danger Strikes Out" and wonder at their difference since both intercessions changed situations, removed danger, and brought peace.

The Shocking Reality of Visions", termed *Situational* Intercession, involves an incident in the *present*, and transpires to change the event as it is *in progress*. "Impending Danger Strikes Out" termed *Preventative* Intercession, involves an incident in the *future*, and transpires to prevent the situation from happening altogether, or to cause it to transpire differently. In other words:

Situational Intercession is **PRESENT TENSE**
Preventative Intercession is **FUTURE TENSE**

When either type of intercession is in progress, the intercessor might not understand which intercession is transpiring, present or future, (situational or preventative). To understand which type is operative, when it is operative, is not important. Remember, intercession is only classified into types to present the topic in an understandable format and to explain the broad spectrum and power of intercession. To help in our understanding of this intercession, let us read about some specific preventative intercession found in the Bible.

BIBLE PREVENTATIVE INTERCESSIONS

Genesis 18:16-33
> [16] And the men rose up from thence, and looked toward Sodom: and Abraham went with them to bring them on the way. [17] And YeHoVaH said, Shall I hide from Abraham that thing which I do; [18] Seeing that Abraham shall surely become a great and mighty nation, and all the nations of the earth shall be blessed in him? [19] For I know him, that he will command his children and his household after him, and they shall keep the way of YeHoVaH, to do justice and judgment; that YeHoVaH may bring upon Abraham that which he hath spoken of him. [20] And YeHoVaH said, Because the cry of Sodom and Gomorrah is great, and because their sin is very grievous; [21] I will go down now, and see whether they have done altogether according to the cry of it, which is come unto me; and if not, I will know.
>
> [22] And the men turned their faces from thence, and went toward Sodom: but Abraham stood yet before YeHoVaH. [23] And Abraham drew near, and said, Wilt

thou also destroy the righteous with the wicked? ²⁴Peradventure there be fifty righteous within the city: wilt thou also destroy and not spare the place for the fifty righteous that are therein? ²⁵That be far from thee to do after this manner, to slay the righteous with the wicked: and that the righteous should be as the wicked, that be far from thee: Shall not the Judge of all the earth do right?

²⁶And YeHoVaH said, If I find in Sodom fifty righteous within the city, then I will spare all the place for their sakes. ²⁷And Abraham answered and said, Behold now, I have taken upon me to speak unto the Lord, which am but dust and ashes: ²⁸Peradventure there shall lack five of the fifty righteous: wilt thou destroy all the city for lack of five? And he said, If I find there forty and five, I will not destroy it.

²⁹And he spake unto him yet again, and said, Peradventure there shall be forty found there. And he said, I will not do it for forty's sake. ³⁰And he said unto him, Oh let not the Lord be angry, and I will speak: Peradventure there shall thirty be found there. And he said, I will not do it, if I find thirty there.

³¹And he said, Behold now, I have taken upon me to speak unto the Lord: Peradventure there shall be twenty found there. And he said, I will not destroy it for twenty's sake. ³²And he said, Oh let not the Lord be angry, and I will speak yet but this once:

> *Peradventure ten shall be found there. And he said, I will not destroy it for ten's sake.* ³³*And YeHoVaH went his way, as soon as he had left communing with Abraham: and Abraham returned unto his place.*

This example of preventative intercession shows YeHoVaH's willingness to stop a city from destruction, and Abraham's intercession to those ends. Due to this intercession Abraham's family members living in Sodom and Gomorrah were saved from destruction, but the city, sorry to say was not. While this intercession did not change the *entire* outcome, it did change the outcome for Abraham's family.

Here is another example of Preventative Intercession

> Exodus 32:9-14
> ⁹*And YeHoVaH said unto Moses, I have seen this people, and, behold, it is a stiffnecked people:* ¹⁰*Now therefore let me alone, that my wrath may wax hot against them, and that I may consume them: and I will make of thee a great nation.*
>
> ¹¹*And Moses besought YeHoVaH his God, and said, YeHoVaH, why doth thy wrath wax hot against thy people, which thou hast brought forth out of the land of Egypt with great power, and with a mighty hand?* ¹²*Wherefore should the Egyptians speak, and say, For mischief did he bring them out, to slay them in the*

> *mountains, and to consume them from the face of the earth?*
>
> *Turn from thy fierce wrath, and repent of this evil against thy people. ¹³Remember Abraham, Isaac, and Israel, thy servants, to whom thou swarest by thine own self, and saidst unto them, I will multiply your seed as the stars of heaven, and all this land that I have spoken of will I give unto your seed, and they shall inherit it for ever. ¹⁴And YeHoVaH repented of the evil which he thought to do unto his people.*

Due to this intercession with Moses, an entire nation was spared. This marvellous example of preventive intercession also clearly demonstrates what happens when an intercessor takes hold of *YeHoVaH's character*.

Both intercessory examples of Moses and Abraham clearly show that Preventative Intercession is biblical. They show the intercessor YeHoVaH's tremendous quality of compassion towards humankind. In addition, these examples demonstrate YeHoVaH's respect to the *covenant relationship* He had with both Abraham and Moses.

As an intercessor, hang on to that! It is a wonderful insight to tuck away! If intercessor grabs hold of the importance of "covenant" in intercession, they will possess a valuable key to have great weight with YeHoVaH. Through the intercession "Impending

Danger Strikes Out", you can recognize both the covenant commitment of YeHoVaH towards my household, and the prevention of a threatening situation.

When I received the factual evidence of the intercession, I was amazed. I could see each detail resembled the intercession, point by point. This doesn't always happen. There are times in preventative intercession when the incident is so completely terminated no record of it will exist, or it might be reduced so much that any appearance of a threat of danger is erased.

Many intercessors have related that prior to September 11th, 2001, *(the day the New York towers fell)* a greater disaster was averted through intercession. Perhaps heaven will one day reveal the many faces of that intercession and others like it, but for now many "preventative intercessory experiences" will transpire with little earthly notice, or often, no notice at all.

It is my belief that our beloved YeHoVaH longs to see intercessors rise in every nation of the world to prevent horrible tragedies such as the one on 9-11. I am firmly convinced that YeHoVaH would prefer to see intercessors increase in number and refine their skills to release His Power into pending disasters, than to see humankind experience such tragedies, which is a good reason to reach out to Him to move into intercession to the deepest limits possible. *Preventative Intercession streams from the heart of YeHoVaH with a passion to be obeyed. Oh, Church! Let us avail ourselves to His Call of Intercession!*

ANALYSIS OF IMPENDING DANGER STRIKES OUT

To receive greater clarity of Preventative Intercession which shows in this chapter's intercession, entitled, Impending Danger strikes out, let us first go through the list of principles explained earlier in other chapters. Following that, we will highlight new ones.

EARLIER PRINCIPLES OF INTERCESSION

1.	**The Lord initiated the intercession**
Yes	*This was another intercession spurred on by a vision.*
2.	**Wait on the Lord for His Leading & Guidance.**
Yes	*I did not assume what this intercession was about, but waited until it was totally revealed. In this way, I waited on the Lord for His leading and guidance.*
3.	**The Holy Spirit partnered with the believer.**
	Once again, the Holy Spirit partnered with me when He presented the vision and gave me the wisdom to intercede.

	4.	The focus was shifted from the situation to the Lord & His ability.
Yes		*The Intercessor & one trucker looked to the Lord.*
	5.	Agreement was made with the Lord.
Yes		*There was active agreement as the intercessor's actions agreed with the Lord's desire for the situation to be altered.*
	6.	God's promises from the Word used as reminders to see them fulfilled.
Yes		*The Word of God was not used by <u>direct</u> quote in the moments of the intercession, but the intercession transpired because of the covenant promises between the Lord and the intercessor.*
	7.	Intercession was made into the direct will of the Lord through groaning.
No		*This principle was not used this time.*
	8.	Intercession was made to the Lord through weeping.
No		*This principle was not used this time.*
	9.	Intercession transpired until a peace came.

Yes	In this case, peace came for the driver and peace came for the intercessor when the vision ended.
10.	**Assurance was given by the Lord, that intercession was complete.**
Yes	*When the vision ended, it was clear the intercession was complete.*
11.	**The Lord gave a word of knowledge.**
Yes	*The word of knowledge included the situation, as well as the word to diffuse the demonic powers fuelling the situation.*
12.	**The vision was prayed into.**
Yes	*This vision was prayed into as it transpired, and until it ended.*
13.	**The Lord responded to the desperate cry.**
Yes	*The desperate cry given by the driver would take place later, in the future, but the Lord responded to it before it was uttered! (Read Psalm 139:3)*
14.	**The Angels of the Lord were sent into the situation.**
No	*(Not used here)*

Having reviewed these principles, let us see what new principles of intercession await our discovery.

Chapter 4 — Impending Danger Strikes Out

NEW PRINCIPLES OF INTERCESSION:

PRINCIPLE # 15

YeHoVaH Broke off the Dangerous Thinking

As you read the Word, you will find that YeHoVaH often challenges humankind to think differently, inviting us to think as He does. YeHoVaH approached Cain to think differently about his brother Abel. Unfortunately, Cain refused. Moses confronted Pharaoh to change his thinking and thus, let YeHoVaH's people go. Pharaoh, as the Bible reveals, refused to do so immediately.

In the intercession with Gary, the trucker trying to pass him made a very bad choice. His approach to the situation was dangerous and jeopardized his life and that of two others.

Even though I pleaded for the offending trucker to "pull back", there was no response. Unknown to me, the spiritual forces around this trucker locked him into a dangerous mindset.

The Holy Spirit knew exactly what was happening. I didn't! I could have *assumed* the driver was trying to commit suicide, or was either overtired or on drugs, but there is no place for assumption in intercession. Assumption can pull you away from the target of the intercession and take you to a place where you will miss the bull's eye! To "assume" is to swing wildly, battering the air, just hoping for good results. This is not a good idea for intercession. Go directly to YeHoVaH for His input, and don't move out, or speak into a situation without it! Stay within YeHoVaH's will. Don't follow assumptions!

After waiting on YeHoVaH, a command with His authority arose out of my spirit. Its release into the situation was a direct hit, causing the offending trucker to immediately pull back, thus defusing the entire situation. I'll address authority in principle # 16, but here it is sufficient to know this: the trucker's thought pattern, fuelled by the adversary, changed immediately after the command was given. Any hold the adversary had on his mind *at that time*, shattered, enabling the man to act rationally. In the end, all three truckers were spared a terrible fate because "the dangerous thinking" was broken off.

PRINCIPLE # 16

Demonic Spiritual Forces commanded to let go

In this intercession, the authoritative command pulled the plug on the demonic powers that were operative and disconnected them from their control of the situation. Demonic forces had already overpowered one person's good sense, causing him to put his own life, and those of two others, in jeopardy.

This plot of the adversary stood in direct contradiction to *YeHoVaH's plan* for my husband's life, for our family and probably for the lives of the others involved. Consequently, YeHoVaH intervened, via an intercession.

> *Isaiah 14:27 says,*
> *For the Lord of hosts hath purposed, and who shall disannul it? And his hand is stretched out, and who shall turn it back?*

REBUKING HA SATAN

Part of the believer's life includes understanding about authority and spiritual warfare. Many books have been written on this subject, so I don't intend to address it. Since this is a book on intercession and its principles, not on Spiritual Warfare[12], I wish only to outline a balance on the subject of "rebuking the adversary".

Let me reiterate the fact that the intercessor (in any type of intercession) must wait for YeHoVaH and carefully obey His promptings. This includes releasing commands of any kind, whether it is sending out warring angels, rebuking the adversary, or giving commands of another nature.

---

[12] *If you don't understand Spiritual Warfare, or the authority in Messiah, ask your pastor to recommend a good book on the subject*

To bring about a fruitful intercession with <u>*full results and not partial*</u>, it is imperative the intercessor stays centered on YeHoVaH's will always, especially when taking the adversary to task. Rebuking the adversary can distract a person, *if they are not careful,* and pull them away from their target. Our adversary is very sly and will try to focus attention on him, or elsewhere.

An intercessor's mind must be fixed on YeHoVaH, waiting to receive His every word. With this mindset, the intercessor remains fully centered on YeHoVaH and speaks forth God's commands. When rebuking the adversary under those conditions, the adversary will not argue or refuse what has been ordered but will obey immediately, not able to sidetrack, confuse or perform any of his antics. This is the desired result, right?

For results that shake the situation free of demonic involvement, always ensure commands echo from the throne room of YeHoVaH. Then, the adversary will have no choice but to cease his operations at once as the commands are released. This is the authority of the believer in action.

> *Matthew 16:19[b]*
> *...whatsoever thou shalt bind on earth shall be bound in heaven: and whatsoever thou shalt loose on earth shall be loosed in heaven.)*

Wait for YeHoVaH to reveal every force that He wants removed. He might not show that all at one time, and maybe not when you want Him to, but the information will come, even if it is spread throughout the intercession. Learn to walk with Him one step at a time. Wait patiently between the steps! It may feel like you are taking "baby steps", but if you learn to take "baby steps" with Him today, you will soon be ready for "giant steps" tomorrow.

When YeHoVaH reveals a demonic spiritual force to you, know this: **Once it is revealed, it is time for it to go!** You use the authority in Messiah[13] and get rid of the adversary along with his plans and his forces. Using the name of Yeshua, separate him from his assignment, command the adversary to let go and speak into the situation where the adversary maintained his stronghold.

Release healing and/or the power of YeHoVaH (whichever is appropriate), and of course, all in accordance with, and in line with, what YeHoVaH has shown you. Don't forget two other powerful weapons of warfare are the blood of Yeshua and the Written Word!

---

[13] *Luke 10:19 Behold, I give unto you power to tread on serpents and scorpions, and over all the power of the enemy: and nothing shall by any means hurt you.*

Revelation 12: 11
¹¹And they overcame him by the blood of the Lamb, and by the word of their testimony; and they loved not their lives unto the death.

Do keep these and other scriptures in mind when you are rebuking the adversary. They can be of great value to you, so use them often and with the authority that comes with your position in Messiah.

THIS CHAPTER'S CONCLUSION:

As we have seen in this chapter, events in people's lives can considerably change through intercession. Intercessors only need to recognize that with the help of YeHoVaH, many situations *will turn around*. Demonically driven situations can be shattered, rendered null and void. Situations influenced by man, can be changed as well.

While YeHoVaH will not violate the choices of man, He is usually willing to speak to them, and He can put influences in place to help them change their thinking. If they refuse to do so, He is still capable of bringing other factors into a situation to help prevent injury to innocent parties and lessen tragedies. Often, all that is required is an intercessor.

Preventative Intercession, presented to an intercessor and kept under the Guidance of the Holy Spirit, is dynamic. It is an invitation for intercessors to enter the activities of intercession and join their waiting Partner Who is willing to teach them whatever they need to know.

DEFINITION:
PREVENTATIVE INTERCESSION

This intercession transpires _before_ an incident occurs. Due to the changes brought about through preventative intercession, an event may appear in a reduced status, or it may manifest differently than originally shown to the intercessor. There may be traces of the event showing the background activities that led up to the event, or even these may be eliminated, so no trace of the event is evidenced at all.

AN EXERCISE TO SPUR ON THE INTERCESSOR

On the following pages you'll find suggestions for *possible intercessions*. If you wish to do this exercise, begin by taking a piece of paper and cover **Box B, without reading it.** Next, read **Box A**. It suggests a possible situation in *preventative* intercession. Think about the situation and write down how *you might respond*. [14]Uncover Box B and read other p*ossible responses* for you to consider *along with* your own suggestions.

(This exercise is only to help you think about intercession, for when in intercession, the Holy Spirit brings forth everything needed.)

---

[14] You will find some space left under each situation just in case you want to write out your thoughts!

POSSIBLE SITUATION # 1

BOX A	An intercessor, *through his or her own life's experience*, recognizes that a problem or situation will occur in someone's life resulting in distress, harm, or death. How could an intercessor respond?
	POSSIBLE RESPONSE
BOX B	Seek YeHoVaH to confirm that your conclusions are correct, verifying what you think could happen, will. Then ask YeHoVaH how to intercede to change the inevitable. Ask YeHoVaH for ways to align that person, and the situation with His will, declare applicable scriptures, prophetic statements, etc. as YeHoVaH releases them to you. *Remember:* YeHoVaH is more than willing to re-align circumstances with His will.

POSSIBLE SITUATION # 2

BOX A	An intercessor receives a *revelation* regarding the future of a person, city, region, or nation. The revelation reveals a situation that will bring death, destruction, or judgment.
	POSSIBLE RESPONSE
BOX B	The intercessor presents the information back to YeHoVaH. If it is about: • *Judgment*: seek YeHoVaH for forgiveness and then, petition YeHoVaH for a delayed, reduced, or averted judgment • *Disasters*: seek YeHoVaH to inquire, what and how it may be averted; ask for "special helps" to be sent into the situation to reduce deaths, etc. • *Situation causing death*: Seek YeHoVaH so you can partner with Him to prevent, or alter the situation so "life" is maintained

POSSIBLE SITUATION # 3

BOX A	An intercessor, through his or her knowledge of the scriptures, recognizes an event is about to be fulfilled, but knows the current events do not line up with the prophetic word.
	POSSIBLE RESPONSE
BOX B	He or she then partners with YeHoVaH to see things are aligned with the "Prophetic Word", pulling events, influences or other things involved, away from a "natural" course and speed it towards YeHoVaH's Plans and Purposes
(It may take quite a while before you are ready to do this, since it will take time and sequenced events in YeHoVaH's realm and earth's, but for now, just know the possibilities exist and be open to it!)	

HOW ARE YOU AT IDENTIFYING THESE PRINCIPLES?

Recognizing the principles of intercession in operation is not a necessity to do your own intercessions. However, learning to recognize the principles helps an intercessor to comfortably use the principle, knowing that it is biblical and that is brings effective fruit!

A WILLING VESSEL

Perhaps, you could take a moment and lay your life out before YeHoVaH, expressing to Him how much you wish to glorify Him *through your life*. If that means He wants you to plunge deep into intercession, tell Him how you feel about doing that. Bare your soul, whether your thoughts are clear about the subject, mixed, or slightly confused. Share with YeHoVaH any reservations, refusals, excuses, doubts, or concerns, along with any expectations or personal hopes. Your

Heavenly Covenant Partner is your friend, and willing to meet you right where you are! If you are a vessel willing for His Glory, He will work out all the details helping you, if necessary, to accept His Will.

CAPTURED BY GOD'S LOVE

In late autumn, on one particular evening I was at home in the shower, praising and blessing YeHoVaH, simply thanking Him for an interesting and full day. Suddenly, the Holy Spirit began to initiate an intercession![15] This intercession had several parts to it, with certain phases to each one.

As the intercession began, I surrendered to YeHoVaH's promptings to groan and weep. I did not know what the intercession[16] was about, but YeHoVaH did. I proceeded to follow YeHoVaH's leading in intercession, while at the same time finish up in the bathroom. I was about to leave the bathroom when YeHoVaH stopped me. For some reason, it was

---

[15] *YeHoVaH doesn't seem to mind the place if we don't!*
[16] *Remember, I call this Blind intercession*

important that this intercession take place right there in the bathroom. (Now the rest of the intercession is a little hard to explain, so please hang in there.)

For the duration of the intercession, it felt like another person was placed over my body. It seemed as if I wore that person like one wear a garment. At this point, the Holy Spirit helped me to see that, *for a while*, I was a *"Substitute"* for a person in need. When this happened, I did not know the person's identity, but I did know the person was a female close to my age and she was unsaved. Feelings of hopelessness and despair overwhelmed her so much that she had attempted to commit suicide by taking an overdose of sleeping pills.

Now that a mental knowledge of the situation had been released, I began to intercede asking YeHoVaH to help the woman remove the ingested pills. That meant she must put her fingers in the back of her throat and induce vomiting. Unfortunately, she resisted the urge.

As the intercession progressed, I knew the woman was so engulfed with feelings of hopelessness, despair, and helplessness, that she felt no one could possibly understand or help her. This intercession was to birth "a cry for help" and "a fight to stay alive". Strength for resistance must also be imparted to her, so she could mentally break her agreement with the spirit of death that drew her into suicide.

A strong battle ensued over her life. She was firmly fixed into an agreement with death, stubbornly resisting the drive to stay alive and the urge to remove the ingested pills. Great opposition arose to any promptings that the Holy Spirit sent her way. She was locked tight to a mindset of her own death.

Sensing urgency in this matter, I continued to intercede, trusting YeHoVaH to give me wisdom to break apart all resistance and establish a surrender to His will so the woman would embrace life. Realizing the strength of the opposition was intense, before I issued commands in the Spirit, I asked YeHoVaH to surround the woman, cradling her in His Arms of Love. I asked Him to reach deep inside of her and touch her inner most being.

This Divine Siege would release His Love, Care and Tenderness to her, thus silencing the voice of rejection and worthlessness. I persisted in this manner until I knew the woman felt the warmth of YeHoVaH's embrace, and I was assured she agreed to be liberated from the oppressing spirit of death. I then issued the necessary commands and asked YeHoVaH, one more time, to help the woman yield to His promptings and remove the pills. This time she agreed and induced a vomit to rid her body of all the pills.

I continued to intercede until the woman agreed to phone someone for help. When she consented to do this, a peace entered my heart, but the feeling of "wearing the person" was still present. At that point, YeHoVaH revealed the person to me. *(Let's call her "Carolyn")* I wanted to race to the phone to call Carolyn, but YeHoVaH advised me to call another person named Debbie.

Debbie was extremely close to Carolyn and would receive a good response from Carolyn. I phoned Debbie at once but of course, I could not reveal the exact details of the intercession due to the private nature of it. I simply told Debbie that, through intercession, I knew that Carolyn experienced a life-threatening situation and that she would call her shortly so the two of them could talk about it. I put down the receiver, and then immediately, the "veiled person" was lifted from me. This intercession ended.

Later, I discovered Debbie had barely placed her receiver back in the cradle when the phone rang. It was Carolyn. She related to Debbie the details of her life-threatening experience. She mentioned taking an overdose of pills to end her life, and she mentioned that she purged them from her system. The happy ending is this: Carolyn was saved from a suicidal attempt and was given strength to resist rejection and despair. She was also given courage to reach out to another for help, embraced by a loving friend who would give her the human support she needed through the following months.

This intercession is termed:
SUBSTITUTE INTERCESSION

In this intercession entitled, "Captured by YeHoVaH's Love", through the power of the Holy Spirit, YeHoVaH had me "wear another person" like a garment. For the short time I was in intercession, I used my knowledge of YeHoVaH and the intercessory skills He gave me to benefit another. In YeHoVaH's eyes, for the duration of the intercession, I was a "stand in" or "substitute" for Carolyn. Therefore, this type of intercession is called: "Substitute Intercession". In this event of Carolyn's averted suicide attempt, the intercession began with the first stage of groaning and weeping and then progressed to the next stage where YeHoVaH made me the stand in, or substitute for Carolyn.

"Substitution" is a recurring principle found throughout the Bible. An excellent example can be found in Genesis 22:9-12. Abraham's most treasured gift, Isaac, the promised child, was to be offered to YeHoVaH as a burnt offering. Out of Isaac's loins, YeHoVaH promised to bring forth a mighty nation with more citizens in number than the stars in the heaven. If Isaac, yet unmarried, became the sacrifice on that altar, *the promise of that nation of people yet to spring forth from his seed,* would become null and void because Isaac's seed would die with him. The account reads:

> Genesis 22:9-12
> *⁹And they came to the place, which God had told him of; and Abraham built an altar there, and laid the wood in order, and bound Isaac his son, and laid him on the altar upon the wood. ¹⁰And Abraham stretched forth his hand, and took the knife to slay his son. ¹¹And the angel of YeHoVaH called unto him out of heaven, and said, Abraham, Abraham: and he said, Here am I. ¹²And he said, Lay not thine hand upon the lad, neither do thou any thing unto him: for now I know that thou fearest God, seeing thou hast not withheld thy son, thine only son from me.*

Isaac did not resist his father's will, but rather he yielded to the purposes that his father had for his life. Abraham trusted YeHoVaH to fulfill His Covenant promises. If YeHoVaH's Plan for Isaac included burning Isaac as a sacrifice upon an altar, then out of the smouldering ashes, YeHoVaH would cause Isaac to rise again. That is what Abraham declared earlier:

> Genesis 22:5
> *⁵And Abraham said unto his young men, Abide ye here with the ass; and I and the lad will go yonder and worship, and come again to you.*

This statement to Abraham's servants was not a lie to hide a devious and secret plot against Isaac, but it was a declaration of Abraham's faith in YeHoVaH's ability to keep His Promises. Abraham believed the servants would witness the return of Isaac from that mountaintop, and Isaac would live to see the fulfillment of YeHoVaH's plans to make him a great nation.

It was probably with great relief in Abraham's heart that his hand was stayed from slaying his son. Great joy most likely filled his heart when he was commanded to spare his son:

> Genesis 22:11-14
> ¹¹*And the angel of YeHoVaH called unto him out of heaven, and said, Abraham, Abraham: and he said, Here am I. ¹²And he said, Lay not thine hand upon the lad, neither do thou any thing unto him: for now I know that thou fearest God, seeing thou hast not withheld thy son, thine only son from me.*
>
> ¹³*And Abraham lifted up his eyes, and looked, and behold behind him a ram caught in a thicket by his horns: and Abraham went and took the ram, and offered him up for a burnt offering in the stead of his son. ¹⁴And Abraham called the name of that place Jehovahjireh: as it is said to this day, In the mount of YeHoVaH it shall be seen.*

Abraham saw the ram caught in the thicket. He then released Isaac from the altar and put the ram on the altar in Isaac's place. Abraham's son would not suffer death because YeHoVaH had provided a SUBSTITUTE for Isaac.

From this scriptural account, we understand that *first*, the ram "replaced" Isaac and it would take the blow of death instead of Isaac. *Secondly*, we understand this account is a picture or prophetic type of Calvary to show us that we, like Isaac, need "a Lamb" to die in our place. After all, the penalty for our sin is death. The Lamb of God, in agreement with the plans of the Father, became our personal substitute when He died on the cross at Calvary.

Yeshua was a *Substitute* for all humanity and through His own life, death, and resurrection, He brought about our marvellous salvation. Our eternal salvation was forever established through the *principle of Substitution*, thus maintaining a full restoration to YeHoVaH. Only our willingness is needed to accept "the substitute" to see salvation realized in our lives.

Salvation is perhaps the most beautiful example of Substitute Intercession within the Word of YeHoVaH, and it is so totally complete, nothing could be added to it nor taken away from it. While *salvation*, through the principle of Substitute Intercession *is finished*, the <u>principle of substitution</u> is not. Its use in the finished work of the cross neither nullified nor prohibited a further use of the *principle of substitution after the cross*. Rather, "Substitute Intercession", by virtue of the principle of substitution, presents a privilege to intercessors to follow in the Master's footsteps.

Of course, no believer can ever be a substitute to pay for another's sins, nor can any believer bring about anyone's healing.

Substitute Intercession, through *the principle of substitution*, presents a divine opportunity to an intercessor to unselfishly plead for another, so YeHoVaH's plans, and purposes can be realized in the life of another person. An intercessor can take full advantage of their established position in Messiah and from that place, intercede for another, so they too can benefit, even if indirectly, from the benefits of the cross.

Substitute Intercession is humanly impossible for any intercessor to initiate. Only YeHoVaH, through the power of the Holy Spirit, can perform the substitution. YeHoVaH's Holy intentions invite His children to a unique identification with their fellow man, as YeHoVaH Yeshua identified with His fellow man. Intercessors, for a moment in time, "stand" in the place of another, to benefit the person in need. YeHoVaH *orchestrates everything,* scheduling the timeframe, initiating, and releasing all that is needed, at every point in the intercession, to bring it to completion.

When YeHoVaH *superimposes another upon an intercessor,* in some way, the intercessor can understand the needs of the person. To recognize the need, some intercessors feel the symptoms of the other person's sickness, or they may feel the physical pain or emotional trauma of the person in need, as these manifest, to some *minor* degree, in the intercessor's body.[17] This is not every intercessor's experience. Some intercessors have sensations on the outside of their body, externally applied to make them aware of the problems.

Those external sensations are intended to make the intercessor aware of the physical pain, symptoms of the sickness, or the emotional traumas of the person in need, but they remain in a protected atmosphere around the intercessor. This has been more my experience. For me, a blanket of peace surrounds me, then, on the outside of my body, I recognize any feelings of pain, sickness symptoms, sorrows, traumas, or whatever else might be involved. These terminate as the intercession finishes.

My reason for detailing Substitute Intercession is not to frighten you, nor is it to turn you off intercession

---

[17]*Normal Grubb, the author of "The Intercessor" (ISBN 087509219X) recorded that during the life of Rees Howell, in doing intercession for a person with tuberculosis, Rees manifested symptoms of the disease, including spitting up blood, but all symptoms left his body when the person was healed.*

either, rather it is to let you know what *can happen* in intercession. Whether or not it happens to you is <u>primarily</u> the choice of the Holy Spirit as He presents it, and <u>secondarily,</u> the choice of the intercessor to accept or refuse it.

If you feel this kind of intercession is not for you, be open with YeHoVaH about it. He will either groom you to accept it, if you are willing, or He will lead you in another direction. As is normal with YeHoVaH, He gives us "free choice" and He will never violate that gift to man.

If you agree and accept this form of intercession, remember, *in Substitute Intercession,* for its duration, *in the eyes of YeHoVaH,* you are standing in for another person in need. Use your faith, your knowledge of the scriptures and of the benefits of the cross, throughout the intercession. Your love for YeHoVaH, and often His Love for the person in need will propel you forward and take you to the finished side of the intercession.

Substitute Intercession is a powerful tool to make a difference in another's life, while at the same time, draws you into a greater appreciation of the YeHoVaH you serve.

At any time, when in any type of intercession, if you feel uncomfortable, take a moment, and speak to

YeHoVaH about this. If need be, He will lift the intercession until you "get your head" around the situation. It is His good pleasure to help you. The Holy Spirit is a very kind, gentle Person, and is most co-operative. He may desire to stretch you in intercession so you can grow, but He'll never give you more than you can handle. He will monitor your progress, ensure your heart beats in tune with His, and He will watch over your timetable. You'll never miss out on anything of eternal value while in intercession.

ANALYSIS OF THIS INTERCESSION
As we have done in other chapters, we will do here. We will review the principles we have learned earlier, mention if they were applicable to the present intercession, and then highlight the New Principles of Intercession operative.

EARLIER PRINCIPLES OF INTERCESSION

1.	**YeHoVaH initiated the intercession.**
Yes	*YeHoVaH initiated the groaning and weeping first, and then He initiated the Substitute Intercession.*
2.	**Wait on YeHoVaH for His Leading & Guidance.**
Yes	*In this intercession, the information was released one step at a time, thus making it easy to wait for YeHoVaH's guidance.*

3.	The Holy Spirit partnered with the believer. (Yes)
4.	The focus was shifted from the situation to YeHoVaH & His ability. (Yes)
5.	Agreement was made with YeHoVaH. (Yes)
6.	YeHoVaH's promises from the Word used as reminders to see them fulfilled.
Not by me but by others	*Saved members of Carolyn's family were holding onto covenant promises for her.*
7.	Intercession was made in the direct will of YeHoVaH through "groaning". (Yes)
8.	Intercession was made to YeHoVaH through weeping. (Yes)
9.	Intercession transpired until a peace came. (Yes)
10.	**Assurance was given by YeHoVaH that intercession was complete.**
Yes	*The assurance did not come at the same time as the peace came. It did not come until the intercession ended, after the phone call was made to Debbie.*
11.	**YeHoVaH gave words of knowledge.**
Yes	*In this intercession, the words of knowledge came when the principle of substitution*

12.	**The vision was prayed into.**
No	No vision here.
13.	**YeHoVaH responded to the desperate cry.**
Not known if there was a desperate cry	*In the beginning, there did not appear to be a cry for help from Carolyn. It is possible she did ask YeHoVaH to help her. I don't know that all I know is that **for Carolyn**, it was necessary for help in that moment of her need and after the intercession, a cry for help to a human being must come. Intercession paved the way.*
14.	**The angels of YeHoVaH were sent into the situation. (No) (Not here)**
15.	**YeHoVaH broke off the dangerous thinking.**
Yes	*Through intercession YeHoVaH broke off Carolyn's agreement with death, and her thinking was changed to embrace life instead.*
16.	**Demonic Spiritual forces commanded to let go.**
Yes	*I did not record the commands, but after Carolyn's agreement with death was*

Above the table:

was enacted. This action of YeHoVaH revealed the mental, emotional, and physical state of Carolyn, as well as her progress and receptivity to YeHoVaH's plans and purposes.

> *broken, then the powers of darkness were driven back when ordered to release her.*

NEW PRINCIPLES OF INTERCESSION

PRINCIPLE # 17

YeHoVaH saw the intercessor as a Substitute for another

As the intercessor, I experienced an action of YeHoVaH where I became a stand in for another. I wore "a female person" on my body, like a person wears a garment. I learned later the person was someone I knew, named Carolyn. As the Substitution took place, I became aware of many details about Carolyn, including the feelings and emotions affecting her at the time. While YeHoVaH exposed Carolyn's emotional trauma and pain, He did not release information about her that was unrelated to the work He intended to do at that point in time. For example, I was never made aware of her "major sins" or "failures". Only information relevant to the intercession was revealed.

In "Captured by YeHoVaH's Love", or Carolyn's intercession, there was an urgency to remove the pills taken in an overdose. A cry for help to a trusted friend was also birthed during the intercession. This established an important connection for an immediate source of help for Carolyn and in addition, provided companionship for her throughout the healing process. That is the reason why the impression of "wearing Carolyn" did not lift until *after* the phone call was made. When I made the phone call, I was still in intercession for the intercession ended after the phone call was completed. Later, I was told the following facts:

- Carolyn took the pills in the bathroom and was there when I was in intercession on her behalf.
- Carolyn wanted to leave the bathroom for her bedroom. There she planned to fall asleep on her bed, hoping she had ingested enough pills to never awaken, <u>*but*</u> she was "prevented" from leaving the bathroom, (just as I was prevented from leaving!)
- Carolyn felt an urge to purge the pills immediately after she had taken the pills, but resisted that urge
- An overwhelming sense of Love suddenly overshadowed Carolyn, and suddenly, *her reasons for suicide* were quieted
- The urge to purge the pills became stronger immediately after she felt her reasons for suicide quiet down. She yielded to the urge and vomited her stomach contents into the toilet.
- Carolyn immediately left the bathroom (the same as I did)
- Carolyn then called her friend (the same one I did)

Wow! Now that is YeHoVaH's awesome power at work!

Carolyn still had some difficult issues to deal with in the future, but these issues had been put in a context of "hope" and not "despair"! She has since received counselling, and in the fifteen years or so since the incident occurred, Carolyn has gone on to do some excellent things with her life, touching many people! Praise YeHoVaH for substitute intercession.

PRINCIPLE # 18
YeHoVaH executed a Divine Siege

In "Captured By YeHoVaH's Love", I wrote: *"I asked YeHoVaH to surround the woman, (Carolyn) cradling her in His Arms of Love. I asked Him to reach deep inside her and touch her inner most being. This Divine Siege would release His Love, Care and Tenderness to her, thus silencing the voice of rejection and worthlessness."*

A Divine Siege surrounds an individual with a purpose like any other siege. First, we'll look at the biblical validity of this principle, and then we'll explain the effects of a Divine Siege.

BIBLICAL VALIDITY:

Isaiah 29: 1-4
¹Woe to Ariel, to Ariel, the city where David dwelt! add ye year to year; let them kill sacrifices. ²Yet I will distress Ariel, and there shall be heaviness and sorrow: and it shall be unto me as Ariel. ³And I will camp

against thee round about, and <u>will lay siege</u> against thee with a mount, and I will raise forts against thee. ⁴And thou shalt be brought down, and shalt speak out of the ground, and thy speech shall be low out of the dust, and thy voice shall be, as of one that hath a familiar spirit, out of the ground, and thy speech shall whisper out of the dust.

Jerusalem, here called Ariel, is promised a siege by YeHoVaH. This siege happened around 70 AD. Rather than go into more detail about this siege in Jerusalem, I would just like to point out what this passage says about the person initiating the siege.

Verse 3 reads *"And I will camp against thee round about, and <u>will lay siege</u> against thee with a mount, and I will raise forts against thee."*

It is YeHoVaH who will perform the siege, encamping around the city and laying a siege, Himself. When the siege happened, an army completed the siege, but what I want you to see here is that YeHoVaH says: *He will lay a siege.*

There was another city where YeHoVaH laid a siege. That one is very familiar to most Bible readers and is a little easier to understand. In the First Covenant, in Joshua Chapter 6, YeHoVaH besieged Jericho, and then, after His Instructions were followed, Joshua physically took the city. Before Jericho's walls crumbled, the armies of Israel surrounded the city for seven days.

This was a typical siege of the day in the sense that the army surrounded the city. It was not typical in the sense that Jericho's walls fell supernaturally, and that, in the early days of the siege. Israel then entered Jericho, after the DIVINE SIEGE prepared the way and removed all that opposed them. A total victory was given to children of Israel because of this Divine Siege orchestrated by YeHoVaH of Hosts.

A Divine Siege, in intercession, has a very similar purpose to the siege at Jericho. Let's look at the intercession in "Captured by YeHoVaH's Love" to analyze the effects of the Divine Siege on Carolyn.

EFFECTS OF A DIVINE SIEGE:
Carolyn was in distress, besieged already with circumstances that "held her captive" to the adversary of her soul. Ha satan[18] oppressed her life with lies and deceptions. When the Divine Siege was enacted, YeHoVaH placed Himself between Carolyn and the adversary, thus cutting off the adversary's power. YeHoVaH then, destroyed the purpose of the adversary to take Carolyn's life.[19]

---

[18] *ha satan, when interpreted means the adversary.*
[19] *For this purpose the Son of God was manifested, that he might destroy the works of the devil. 1John 3:8*

This tender embrace of love from the Almighty silenced the voices of rejection and worthlessness speaking into Carolyn's life, thus freeing her to make a sensible decision in favour of living. After the Divine Siege, Carolyn purged her system of the pills, and in time to prevent any side effects or damage from the pills. This Divine Siege demonstrates a wonderful principle of intercession, to cut off adversary supplies and invade a life with the love of YeHoVaH.

One last point: if an intercessor is face-to-face with a person in need and YeHoVaH desires a Divine Siege to be implemented, He may do it directly, or He may ask the intercessor to wrap *their arms of love* around the person in need. A hug from an intercessor, filled with the pure essence of YeHoVaH's love, can become a siege to break adversary resistance and demonstrate YeHoVaH's Love.

PRINCIPLE # 19
YeHoVaH revealed hidden information

(Job 15:11b)
   [11] ... *is there any secret thing with thee?*

(Deuteronomy 29:29)
   [29]*The secret things belong unto YeHoVaH*

Hidden information is revealed to an intercessor for a purpose. Normally, that purpose is to enable specific or "targeted intercession" to take place. Exposing "hidden information" takes the "power" out of a situation, making it very accessible and vulnerable to an attack.

When the exposure reveals any demonic activity behind the situation or any demonic strongholds used to entangle or cause havoc in a situation, the intercessor has been given the target and can then go for it ensuring first, exact directions are received from YeHoVaH on just how to proceed.

No two situations are alike, and usually, the solution or commands for one situation, while similar may not be identical. *(See "Rebuking the Adversary" in the chapter "Impending Danger Strikes Out.")*

In this intercession with Carolyn, to prevent her from killing herself, YeHoVaH needed to expose what was going on behind closed doors in Carolyn's home, revealing Carolyn's "secret" activity. Some feelings and emotions were also revealed. These became "red flags" and marked important strongholds that fixed Carolyn to the goal of suicide.

While YeHoVaH did not reveal *everything* oppressing Carolyn, He did reveal enough to show there was *a root problem*. Most often, complex situations will stem from a "root problem", as it did in Carolyn's situation, but it might not be possible for the entire "root" to be removed. In this intercession, YeHoVaH did not intend to unravel all the complex details of Carolyn's life, nor pull the root out, then. He planned to "cut their influence" from Carolyn and bring her to a place where she would face them, and deal with them. He did that by a Siege of Love.

ROOT PROBLEMS IN INTERCESSION:
Root problems in intercession may be removed if ordered by YeHoVaH, but I like to remember advice YeHoVaH recorded for us in the Word:

> Deuteronomy 7: 22-24
> [22]And YeHoVaH thy God will put out those nations before thee by little and little: thou mayest not consume them at once, lest the beasts of the field increase upon thee. [23]But YeHoVaH thy God shall deliver them unto thee, and shall destroy them with a mighty destruction, until they be destroyed. [24]And he shall deliver their kings into thine hand, and thou shalt destroy their name from under heaven: there shall no man be able to stand before thee, until thou have destroyed them.

As an intercessor taught by YeHoVaH on how to deal with "root problems" in intercession, I take this to mean that YeHoVaH will give the victory to the person, *little by little,* as they are able to maintain it. In other words, each "root" is pulled out "one by one" so they can maintain the victory and keep on maintaining it until the entire battle has been won. In my thinking, a little victory that can be maintained is far better than a larger victory that would be soon lost. Yeshua put it another way in Matthew:

Matthew 12: 43-45
⁴³ When the unclean spirit is gone out of a man, he walketh through dry places, seeking rest, and findeth none. ⁴⁴Then he saith, I will return into my house from whence I came out; and when he is come, he findeth it empty, swept, and garnished. ⁴⁵Then goeth he, and taketh with himself seven other spirits more wicked than himself, and they enter in and dwell there: and the last state of that man is worse than the first. Even so shall it be also unto this wicked generation.

Who wants to put anyone in that vulnerable state? Rather than jeopardize another's future, I proceed with caution, removing "root problems" only as I am told to do. I stay within the parameters of my assignment, rather than press past their borders and produce a result other than YeHoVaH's perfect will. This is how YeHoVaH has taught me, and I find it works well for me. I hope this advice works well for you too.

PRINCIPLE 19 EXPANDED:
When interceding for cities, regions or nations, *time* may not usually be as crucial as it was in Carolyn's

case. YeHoVaH, for purposes of any given intercession, may reveal "Root causes" supernaturally, and/or lead one into a YeHoVaH-ordained study of a region by natural investigation to bring about His will in this regard, *and* YeHoVaH may release a strategy to "topple" these "root causes" quickly, but most often they are uprooted slowly.

Everything depends upon both how YeHoVaH wants the information used and His timeframe. Many intricate factors or root causes in one region may connect with intricate factors and causes in other regions. They may affect an entire nation. A domino affect often occurs when an entire root system is pulled out. Only YeHoVaH knows which "domino" to remove to produce the overall affect needed for the season and the fulfillment of His overall plans and purposes.

Add to this thought another important fact. YeHoVaH has intercessors, most of them unknown to each other, at work side by side *with Him* in specific intercessory activities. These intercessions often parallel each other, complement each other, and are aimed at attaining the same ends. Often, they are designed to unravel or break apart principalities and powers of the air, and then with YeHoVaH's wisdom, intercede for the reconstruction to implement the expansion of the Kingdom of YeHoVaH. That is the usual manner of intercession for cities, regions[20] and nations, since YeHoVaH often selects a team of intercessors to complete large projects. This is only one more reason to walk within the parameters of our own assignment, fulfilling our part in the team effort, even if we don't know our teammates!

AN INTERCESSOR'S DEVELOPMENT
While I do not intend to discuss in detail the various stages of an intercessor's development, I do want to mention the possibilities that await the serious intercessor. Much work is yet to be done in intercession throughout the world and YeHoVaH is busy grooming intercessors to take their part in this great work.

We are privileged to know a few intercessors, since YeHoVaH has revealed them to us, so we may learn and be encouraged by them. Most intercessors, however, are hidden away in the secret place, learning, and growing in their call. Wherever an intercessor fits into the overall picture, you can be sure that they are grown in stages, one step at a time.

Each intercessor usually learns on a smaller scale first, then things are expanded on a larger scale, and of course, information is added as it can be managed by that intercessor. An intercessor must be careful not to

---

[20] *"Region" refers to any area such as a province, territory, or state, etc.*

limit either the power of the Spirit to work through them, His chosen vessel, or the opportunities presented for growth. All ideas of limits in intercession must be removed, falling like the wall of Jericho, before the intercessor can grasp the limitless power to be released in intercession.

THIS CHAPTER'S CONCLUSIONS
"Captured by YeHoVaH's Love" combined two intercessory types together. While the body of the intercession was Substitute Intercession, as the intercession progressed, Situational Intercession united with Substitute Intercession to form a powerful combination to save Carolyn's life.

Substitute Intercession on Carolyn's behalf demonstrated the immense ability of YeHoVaH to love everyone, *especially* those who are overwhelmed with the various aspects of life and traps of ha satan.

Our YeHoVaH's heart pumps with compassion for the underprivileged in every place and circumstance where they can be found. With equal passion and empathy, YeHoVaH invites His children to walk with Him through intercession to bring relief to others in need. An experience of great value, beyond earth's diamonds, awaits any intercessor willing to be "touched" by the Holy Spirit and "moulded" into an intercessor, using this or any other type of intercession.

DEFINITION:
SUBSTITUTE INTERCESSION

As a type of intercession, Substitute Intercession carries out, through the power of the Holy Spirit, the biblical principle for *substitution* throughout *the entire intercession* and enables an intercessor to be seen, in the eyes of YeHoVaH, as a substitute for someone else. Manifestations, like the person in need, may be superimposed upon the intercessor, which in turn, uses their own knowledge of Scripture and of the benefits of the cross to bring victory into the situation as they complete the intercession.

CONFIDENTIALITY IN INTERCESSION

As you can see by this last intercession with Carolyn, intercessors can receive privileged information during intercession.

Privileged information of a very private and personal nature must be kept confidential.

Intimate and personal information is not to be revealed to anyone, not the person on whose behalf the intercession transpired, and certainly not to any other person <u>unless</u> YeHoVaH specifically requests it.

In the intercession with Carolyn, confidential information was entrusted to me continually throughout the intercession. As the intercession neared its end, I was instructed to call Debbie, a friend of Carolyn's. This phone call had two purposes. One, it was part of the substitute intercession, *and two*, the phone call validated Debbie as YeHoVaH's choice to walk with Carolyn on the long journey to full healing.

When I spoke with Debbie, I gave her a broad statement about Carolyn, which could have applied to many circumstances. *Intimate* details of the incident were *not revealed* to Debbie.[21] In this way, Carolyn's privacy was maintained. Carolyn, in her initial contact with Debbie, and throughout the healing process, retains the right to expose information, as she desires. This was not the job of the intercessor.

Of course, not all intercession contains highly sensitive information like the one for Carolyn. In the cases of Jeff *(The Shocking Reality of Visions)* and Gary *(Impending Danger Strikes Out)*, the intercession did not contain material of a highly sensitive nature, so to speak to them about the intercession did not embarrass them but pleased them. Each one was re-affirmed in the fact that YeHoVaH was interested in them and listened to their cries for help.

In conclusion, when speaking about intercession activities, ensure the release of the information will

---

[21] *They have not been revealed in this book either*

glorify YeHoVaH, and not contain any highly sensitive issues that would violate another's privacy. After all, if YeHoVaH trusts you with intimate and personal information in intercession, He trusts you to keep a confidence as well.

BEFORE "CARRIED ON MAJESTIC WINGS"

I ask that you *prayerfully* read the precious truths in this next chapter. Many intercessors experience these treasures of the kingdom, as they are available for the serious intercessor. This next intercession includes a biblical principle we call "transportation". Transportation happens as the Holy Spirit supernaturally takes a person from one place to another. Philip, the apostle, was caught up by the Spirit and transported in such a fashion:

> Acts 8:39-40
> ³⁹And when they were come up out of the water, the Spirit of the Lord caught away Philip, that the eunuch saw him no more: and he went on his way rejoicing. ⁴⁰But Philip was found at Azotus: and passing through he preached in all the cities, till he came to Caesarea.

In "Carried on Majestic Wings", YeHoVaH initiated a Substitute Intercession positioning the intercessor as "a stand in" for an entire family, *and at the same time*, He transported the intercessor with an action that prophetically "carried" an entire family through a very tragic event. *Please* treat the information with respect and give glory to YeHoVaH for His Mighty Hand of Power.

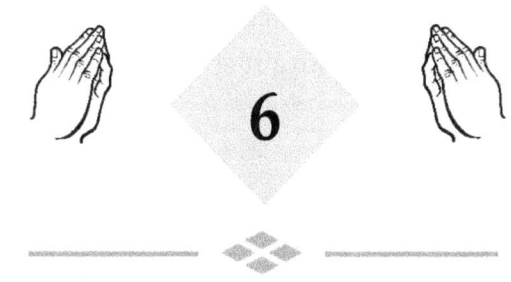

6

CARRIED ON MAJESTIC WINGS

Early on this summer morning, I was reflecting on something that happened the previous evening. I had been visiting an older woman, a believer named Eleanor. After my visit with her, I got into my car and began the **fifteen-minute** drive home. Within moments of leaving Eleanor's driveway, I was at the stoplight on the street near my house. Continuing to drive to my home, I turned into my driveway, and then looked at my watch. Only **five minutes** had passed from the time I left Eleanor's place and pulled into mine. Obviously, **YeHoVaH** had transported me. Although, at this time, He did not convey why He had done this, I knew I would understand later.

On the next morning, a woman named Sandra came to see me. We visited for a while, and then I paused to pray with her. It was in those quiet moments that **YeHoVaH** nudged me to check my phone messages. A little surprised by the instruction, but certain it was **YeHoVaH**, I asked Sandra if she would excuse me for a moment.

Walking towards my answering machine, I remembered that I had taken our dog for a walk before Sandra came, and upon my return home, I did not check for messages. When I checked my answering machine, I decided to answer only those marked urgent. Since one was marked urgent, I listened to it. Eleanor, (the older woman I visited the night before) had left the urgent message. Her words were strained as she related an alarming situation about her grandson, Anthony. "They have taken Anthony [22] to the hospital, forty-five minutes away. *They don't expect him to live.* I'm on my way there now. I'll call you when I can."

Anthony, Eleanor's grandson, was a strapping young man in his late twenties, in reasonably good health. There was no logical reason for him to be rushed to the hospital with such a hopeless prognosis. Since the hospital where Anthony was taken was a fair distance

---

[22] *Not real name*

away, I knew it would be a while before I would have any details about the incident.

Then, the Holy Spirit spoke to me. *"Just as I carried (transported) you last evening, I will transport all of Eleanor's family over the next few days."* This urgent need in Eleanor's family was an intercession **YeHoVaH** intended for me to complete, and in fact, He had begun that intercession the night before. I just didn't know it!

Since the urgent need was not confidential, and Sandra was an intercessor, I shared the message with her. We agreed to put our earlier agenda aside until later and began to pray. As we sought **YeHoVaH** for counsel, the Holy Spirit dropped **a word of knowledge** into my spirit, advising me that *Anthony's lungs* were filled with *"carbon monoxide"* and he needed *"breath"*. *To me that meant that although Anthony was facing death,* **YeHoVaH** *wanted to give him His "breath of life" to keep him alive.*

From that word of knowledge, we began to speak "**YeHoVaH**'s breath" over Anthony, asking the Holy Spirit to sustain him. We included a request for "air" to enter his lungs and petitioned **YeHoVaH** to remove the poisonous gas and all its effects. As we called upon the name of **YeHoVaH** for Anthony's life, we both received this scripture: *"He shall not die but live and declare the works of* **YeHoVaH**.*"*[23]

Compelled by **YeHoVaH**'s counsel, we joined our hearts to release the plan of **YeHoVaH** into the situation and locked into a firm commitment *not* to let Anthony go into the jaws of death. We used the authority in the Name of Yeshua as we entered a spiritual battle to push back the forces of death encompassing Anthony.

There was a pause in the intercession, so I took this opportunity to phone the hospital. I asked to speak with someone in Anthony's family. His mother, Betty, came to the phone. She explained the situation as best as can be expected between the tears and the sobbing. She related that Anthony was exposed to an overwhelming amount of carbon monoxide gas. He was nearly dead from the fumes.

He was given mouth-to-mouth resuscitation immediately at the scene where the incident occurred, and when the ambulance arrived, he was put on oxygen. At his arrival at the hospital, when they measured his blood levels for the concentration of poisonous gas, they found it measured 85% carbon monoxide, and that was after 45 minutes or so of pure

---

[23] *Psalm 118:17   I shall not die, but live, and declare the works of YeHoVaH*

oxygen. They could only imagine how much poison was in his system before the ambulance attendants arrived and gave Anthony oxygen.

At the hospital, the doctors related to Betty that with the level of carbon monoxide in Anthony, he should be dead, and they didn't understand why he was still alive. They gave him no hope of recovery. From their diagnosis, they concluded that the amount of poisonous fumes received in his system would be more than enough to cause severe brain damage, and by some strange hand of fate, if he should live, he would be a "vegetable" the remainder of his life. It would be a blessing if he died. In the interest of preserving his life, they told Betty, there was a special chamber in another hospital, in another city.

This chamber had been designed specifically to assist victims of carbon monoxide poisoning. *If* the chamber was available, it was questionable if Anthony would even survive the transfer to the other hospital. Anthony's mother informed me that the hospital would check on the chamber's availability *only* if she wanted to go that route, but the chamber was no guarantee that Anthony would live. His chance of survival was 2% with the chamber, and 0% without it.

His mother exclaimed with great agony in her voice: "I don't know what to do. Perhaps I should let him go. What if he recovers and is a vegetable? He would not thank me. He would not want to live like that. Yet, if I don't do it, I'll feel I'd robbed him of a chance at life." My heart was moved as I listened to the agony in her voice as she outlined the desperate situation. I knew Betty did not have a personal relationship with the Lord Yeshua, and without this, she would be well past her limits of human endurance.

My comments to Betty were brief, encouraging her to use the best medical knowledge available to preserve his life. I inquired if she would like me to come to the hospital, but Betty related she did not want me to do that at this point. As I ended the conversation and hung up the receiver, I prayed that Eleanor's arrival at the hospital would be expedited, and that **YeHoVaH** would give her wisdom and strength to comfort her family.

Armed with current information, Sandra and I returned for further intercessory activity. Together we praised **YeHoVaH** for the Word of Knowledge He had given to us earlier. We realized also that He had given us wisdom to intercede into a totally unknown situation. Thanks to Divine Intervention and the breath of the Holy Spirit, Anthony was still living, even though it was medically impossible!

Then, we petitioned heaven to change this horrible situation. We locked into an agreement with **YeHoVaH** that He would move mightily in this situation restoring Anthony to life with a fully functioning brain and body.

Although we believed **YeHoVaH** would do that with or without that special carbon monoxide chamber, we petitioned **YeHoVaH** to make it available *to ease Betty's anxiety a little* and give her *some medical hope* she could trust; and furthermore, we asked **YeHoVaH** to speak to Betty, to accept the chamber's use as a viable option.

A chamber did become available and without hesitation, it was accepted. Anthony was transferred to another hospital where the chamber was located. He survived the transfer and immediately upon arrival at the new hospital, he was placed in the chamber.

Anthony's mother, Betty, was grateful for the chamber's availability since that gave her a small ray of hope, but she was still deeply concerned. She became increasingly agitated by the thoughts of her son suffering tremendous brain damage, but at this point, Eleanor, her mother, was at her side expressing love and compassion to her.

YeHoVaH infused a strong faith in the grandmother's spirit, and it was so strong that, at one point, prior to Anthony's entrance in the chamber, where he would be isolated from all human beings, his grandmother grabbed his arm simply to touch him. Anthony's body jumped as if a bolt of electricity had gone through him.

Eleanor boldly proclaimed to Anthony: *"You are not going to die, but live"*. His grandmother spoke over Anthony *the same words* we were speaking over his life in the prayer closet many miles away, and furthermore, she was a vessel anointed by the Holy Spirit to impart **YeHoVaH**'s healing power into Anthony's weakened body. Even though the medical profession continued to advise the family not to get their hopes up, Eleanor believed Anthony would live.

They could only leave Anthony in the carbon monoxide chamber for 48 hours, and then they would have to remove him. Should he still be alive at that point, it was no guarantee he would survive outside the chamber. He might die within the following 48 hours since that was the fate of most victims.

According to the medical doctors, such intense carbon monoxide poisoning meant little to no hope of recovery. After they placed Anthony in the isolation chamber, the doctors sent the family home.

Meanwhile at my home, Sandra had left, promising to intercede as much as her lifestyle permitted. I thanked her for her help and continued support to Eleanor's family and I remained in an attitude of prayer. As I sat on the chesterfield in my living room, my eyes began to fill with tears.

My emotions were moved deeply for Anthony, his grandmother Eleanor, his mother, Betty, and all their family. I began to weep and cry from the depths of my spirit, reiterating to **YeHoVaH** promises that came to my mind, including His covenant relationship with the family.

"You have promised: only believe and you and your household will be saved! *(Acts 16:31* I know Anthony is not saved **YeHoVaH**, so continue to unfold Your Plan to snatch him from the jaws of death!"

I knew there was more intercession yet to be done before **YeHoVaH**'s Plan for this situation would be totally released, but at this point, a deep peace entered my spirit, reaffirming **YeHoVaH**'s divine directive for Anthony's life and complete recovery. **YeHoVaH** knew what was ahead for me that day.

As I went about some chores, *negative* thoughts raced through my mind regarding Anthony's survival. I settled back into that "deep peace" in my spirit given to me earlier. Then I rebuked those negative thoughts!

I declared spiritual affirmations one more time: "Anthony shall not die but live and declare the works of **YeHoVaH**."

Later, in the middle of the night, I was awakened by **YeHoVaH** to continue the intercession for Anthony. I reached out my hands to **YeHoVaH** in praise as His Spirit filled the room where I slept. The Power Source and Author of Life engaged in deep conversation with my spirit. There, from that place in my bedroom, beneath the Shadow of the Almighty, I began to spout orders like a five star General. Authoritative words straight from the throne room of heaven were directed to the spirit of death, commanding him to leave Anthony.

With those words, uttered under the power and fire of the Holy Ghost, the spirit of death immediately was cut away from its assignment against Anthony. **YeHoVaH** gave me a witness that these commands would "immediately" become effective, and I knew Anthony was *not only* going to make it, but **YeHoVaH** would heal his mind and any side effects of the poison. In addition, I had an affirmation that one day, Anthony, along with his whole family, would come to serve **YeHoVaH**.

Morning came and my plans for ministry for that day included a prearranged appointment to take Eleanor to the hospital to visit Anthony. As we travelled to the hospital, Eleanor related how the members of her family and some medical personnel perceived her the day before. They were concerned for her, insisting she was denying reality and would be unable to cope with the loss when Anthony died. Eleanor's faith, however, did not cave in that day and it would not give way today either. Our conversation, throughout that journey to the hospital, would only speak of Anthony's complete and expected recovery.

Eleanor and I arrived at the hospital and joined Anthony's family members, as they gathered around an information station, inquiring as to Anthony's whereabouts. Anthony had been removed from the chamber during the night, and his family wanted to know what happened. Some family members felt this meant Anthony had died in the night, but soon medical staff related to them that, during the middle of the night, Anthony came "back to life". Able to breathe on his own now, he had been placed in a private room on another floor! (Hallelujah!)

Excited by the news, Anthony's family walked to the new waiting room on the floor where Anthony had been transferred. They were eager for a chance to visit with him. The nurse cautioned that each visit could last only a few minutes and if Anthony tired, the visits would have to stop altogether. With so many family members present, I hoped Anthony wouldn't tire before I could visit him.

As I sat in the waiting room with the family, I felt the atmosphere was very strained. Although the family members were all delighted that Anthony had been removed from the chamber, the doctors continued to relate again that they should not get their hopes up yet.

They reminded the family that Anthony might not survive outside the chamber and that brain damage was inevitable. They were sure he would not be the Anthony they knew before! As I sat there, the family spoke very little, pensive once more about the outcome: Would Anthony live outside the chamber? Would he be mentally incapacitated? What would his life be like now?

The nurse finally gave the go ahead for family members to begin their visits. First, the mother, Betty, went in, then the grandmother, Eleanor. After that, they extended an invitation for me to see Anthony, the other family members in full agreement that I should go ahead of them. As I walked towards Anthony's room, I asked **YeHoVaH** for His wisdom to say and do whatever was best for the situation. As I entered the room my heart was moved to tears as I saw Anthony reclining almost lifelessly on the bed with his arms resting by his side. His mother was close to his bedside, not willing to leave him for even a moment.

After greeting the mother, I approached the head of Anthony's bed to speak with him. I bent forward to talk softly into his ear, but I was taken by surprise as Anthony positioned his two arms behind my head, and with an unexpected strength, pulled me towards his face. Anthony wanted my head near his lips. He whispered to me what he did not want others to hear. He said, with tears in his eyes and a cracking voice: "Thanks! You prayed me back from the dead!"

Once more, I was surprised. Anthony knew the source of his return to life was "answered prayer". I whispered back to Anthony comments that reaffirmed his belief that **YeHoVaH** had returned his life to him. I reassured Anthony that **YeHoVaH** loved him and related to him that many people had prayed for him. I assured him that he would not have any brain damage from the poisonous gas and that **YeHoVaH** had a plan for his life that was wonderful.

Within a few short weeks, Anthony was able to walk out of that hospital. His mental capabilities were not damaged in the least little bit and his lungs were perfectly healthy. The hospital staff was astounded at Anthony's recovery, amazed that this close encounter with death had such a happy ending. They remarked many times, how things transpired with everything in place, just when Anthony needed it. They felt Anthony's remarkable recovery was a miracle.

Indeed, Anthony had escaped the jaws of death, the grave and the eternal destination of darkness that awaited him in his unsaved condition. Anthony still needs to know Yeshua as Saviour, but this event in his life does have a happy ending because the Lord God Almighty is a covenant keeping **YeHoVaH**.

> Acts 16: 30-31:
> *"And brought them out, and said, Sirs, what must I do to be saved? ³¹And they said, Believe on the Lord Jesus Christ, and thou shalt be saved, and thy house."*

Anthony, in secular terminology, beat the odds, but to the Christian, ***there are "no odds"*** when you call upon the One who made the heavens and the earth! He overrules all the odds!

Yeshua Ha Mashiach, the living YeHoVaH, is neither limited by death, nor the grasp of it! He conquered it on our behalf and one day, when He gives that shout from His Kingdom, all will arise, those living and those buried beneath the earth! Our **YeHoVaH** is not limited to operate in the realm of this world, but rather, He is limitless in His scope and higher than all elements and powers that exist in the world where we presently live!

We, His children, need to learn and understand how He intends us to walk with Him on this earth, releasing His Authority over all things, literally changing situations and circumstances to reflect His Love and Power. As believers, we need to grab a hold of a knowledge of our **YeHoVaH**, so situations like that of

Anthony's become commonplace, no less appreciated, of course, but commonplace occurrences in the lives of those that love and serve the Almighty.

Revelation 5: 12 b
Worthy is the Lamb that was slain to receive power, and riches, and wisdom, and strength, and honour, and glory, and blessing.

This intercession is termed:
TRANSPORTATIONAL INTERCESSION

There are two types of Transportational Intercession, so we will identify this one as *TYPE A*.

- In TYPE A Transportational Intercession:
  YeHoVaH carries people over traumas, through storms and other times of trouble as He prophetically carried an intercessor.

While we won't discuss TYPE B until later, here is a quick recap:
- In TYPE B Transportational Intercession:
  YeHoVaH carries an intercessor into another place *where intercession takes place*, and then the intercessor is returned.

TRANSPORTATIONAL INTERCESSION TYPE A

Before this chapter, I gave a biblical passage for "transportation", quoting the book of Acts 8: 39-40. The transportation of Philip occurred at the end of a divine moment in time when **YeHoVaH** presented an Ethiopian convert to Judaism with an opportunity for salvation. With the Ethiopian's acceptance of salvation and his baptism complete, Philip was whisked away. While the Ethiopian continued towards his destination of Gaza, Philip was found at Azotus, about thirty miles from the eunuch's destination.

This situation was truly a rare moment in time where **YeHoVaH** acted in a most unpredictable manner, but then again, what we think is unpredictable may well be normal activity for **YeHoVaH**!

Who can define the parameters of **YeHoVaH**, especially regarding how far He'll go to save a soul?

Who can understand the depths of the Holy Spirit's workings?

We serve an awesome **YeHoVaH** with power and abilities far beyond our understanding. The story of the Ethiopian eunuch and the evangelist, Philip, is but a small display of the Love of **YeHoVaH** for the lost. So too is Anthony's intercession, as it indicates **YeHoVaH**'s love and mercy beyond our comprehension.

ANALYSIS OF THIS INTERCESSION

As we review the principles of intercession taught in earlier chapters, unless the principle used *is not too obvious*, we will not explain how it was used.

EARLIER PRINCIPLES OF INTERCESSION

1.	YeHoVaH initiated the intercession. (Yes)
2.	Wait on YeHoVaH for His Leading & Guidance. (Yes)
3.	The Holy Spirit partnered with the believer. (Yes)
4.	The focus was shifted from the situation to YeHoVaH & His ability. (Yes)
5.	Agreement was made with YeHoVaH. (Yes)
6.	YeHoVaH's promises from the Word used as reminders to see them fulfilled. (Yes)
7.	Intercession was made in the direct will of YeHoVaH through "groaning". (No)
8.	Intercession was made to YeHoVaH through weeping. (Yes)
9.	Intercession transpired until a peace came. (Yes)
10.	Assurance was given by YeHoVaH that intercession was complete.
Yes	*At each stage assurance was given.*
11.	YeHoVaH gave words of knowledge.
Yes	*Carbon monoxide poisoning was revealed prior to being told.*
12.	The vision was prayed into. (No Vision)
13.	YeHoVaH responded to the desperate cry.

Yes	*The entire situation could be seen as a desperate cry.*
14.	**The angels of YeHoVaH were sent into the situation. (No)**
15.	**YeHoVaH broke off the dangerous thinking.**
No	YeHoVaH *helped the mother to think clearly.*
16.	**Demonic Spiritual forces commanded to let go.**
Yes	*The Spirit of death was commanded to let Anthony go during the intercession in the evening hours.*
17.	**YeHoVaH saw the intercessor as a substitute for another.**
Yes	*The intercessor was seen as a substitute for Anthony and his family.*
18.	**YeHoVaH enacted a Divine Siege. (No)**
19.	**YeHoVaH revealed Hidden Information. (Yes)**

Before we look at New Principles used, I would like to **add to principle # 6. YeHoVaH***'s promises from the Word were used as reminders to see them fulfilled.* That was certainly an important part of Anthony's intercession, however, *there is factor in this principle* of equal importance. It is this:

YeHoVaH's Word was spoken directly into the situation: "You shall not die but live and declare the works of **YeHoVaH**"!

YeHoVaH's Word in any situation acts like a powerful thunderbolt that shatters the works of darkness! **YeHoVaH's Word** has components in it that no other word contains:

> Jeremiah 23: 29
> ²⁹*Is not my word like as a fire? saith YeHoVaH; and like a hammer that breaketh the rock in pieces?*

Speak the Word of YeHoVaH **directly into any intercession** and remember the above components of the Word. Don't forget this one either:

> Isaiah 55: 11
> ¹¹*So shall my word be that goeth forth out of my mouth: it shall not return unto me void, but it shall accomplish that which I please, and it shall prosper in the thing whereto I sent it.*

Principle # 6 from this point on reads:

PRINCIPLE # 6 Expanded

YeHoVaH's Promises from the Word used as reminders to see them fulfilled and was declared into the situation to change it

Now, let's see what new principles are operative in "Carried on Majestic Wings"

NEW PRINCIPLES OF INTERCESSION

PRINCIPLE # 20
YeHoVaH initiated a transportation

When **YeHoVaH** began the intercession, He saw the intercessor as a Substitute for the family, and then began the transport.

- **THE INTERCESSOR TRANSPORTED**
  This intercessor, seen as a Substitute for the family, was lifted and carried many miles. This transport took place after dark, over a stretch of land mostly without streetlights. In a like manner, **YeHoVaH** would carry Anthony and his family over the next few days through a time of darkness that filled their life.

- **THE GRANDMOTHER TRANSPORTED**
  She was transported as she was borne along <u>by an implanted faith, given to her just for that time</u>. Eleanor relates the night before Anthony's trauma, moments after I left her home, she felt a strong urge to ask **YeHoVaH** to grant her "mustard seed" faith. She had never prayed that prayer before and was surprised that it came so quickly. Eleanor never wavered nor doubted; never gave up, nor, in her own words, "fell apart". Even when the medical people and her kindly family members insisted that she was in a state of denial, she held fast to her faith.

She remarked later *she felt carried over the trauma*. She looked back and wondered with amazement at the strength, energy, and fortitude she had. She was borne along by the Holy Ghost, who carried her above the circumstances.

- **THE MOTHER TRANSPORTED**
  No one will ever know the agony or stress of those moments as the mother faced this situation, but she has remarked how she felt "carried over those dark days"! She doesn't yet know it, but she too was borne along by the Holy Ghost *through intercession*!

- **ALL RESCUE OPERATIONS CONNECTED**
  Throughout the incident, everything connected like clockwork. On the scene, mouth to mouth resuscitation was given to Anthony; an ambulance was immediately available, which was most unusual for that area; the first hospital had a list of available items lined up, ready for Anthony's care; and the second hospital had the rare availability of the chamber for carbon monoxide victims.

- **ANTHONY TRANSPORTED**
  YeHoVaH elevated Anthony above the circumstance while His breath kept Anthony alive. His power surged through Anthony's body before he entered the chamber. His power cut off the spirit of death, thus ending ha satan's assignment; and YeHoVaH Power restored Anthony to life.

YeHoVaH carried Anthony from a state of death, through a horrible trauma, and gently placed him alive on the other side. Anthony commented that he had been prayed back from the dead. Indeed, **YeHoVaH** carried Anthony through the corridor leading to death and brought him back through a narrow passageway to life. Unbelievable! IMPOSSIBLE, but, nevertheless, true!

INTERCESSION OFTEN TRANSPORTS:
In the truest sense of the word, Intercession often "transports", both the intercessor and the subject or subjects within the intercession. One moment, as an intercessor, you begin the intercession, standing, as it were, on the one side of the circumstance. Then the Holy Ghost enters, and the intercession progresses and becomes like a spiritual bridge, brought for you to walk upon and then, walk over until you reach the other side.

Those upheld in intercession also experience the same marvellous transport, but perhaps much less obvious. When looking back, people wonder with amazement how they ever handled such things. How many people do you know that would tell you about a stressful or trying situation they experienced, where they felt carried along? How many of these people were carried by **YeHoVaH**, unaware of His help?

Anthony's situation details *only one* of many incidents. I could relate many more incidents to you, and I'm sure you could relate many to me, where humans were carried as it were, through (or even above) their circumstances! **YeHoVaH** intervenes more often than we can imagine, carrying people on His Majestic wings, through more difficult places than we could ever suppose possible. In fact, He has even carried a nation on His Majestic Wings.

Exodus 19: 4
⁴Ye have seen what I did unto the Egyptians, and how I bare you on eagles' wings, and brought you unto myself.

Israel's population at this time was estimated as two and one half million people. Everyone was carried out of Egypt on the wings of **YeHoVaH** and there was not a sick person among them. I wonder how many knew they were being carried through the planned exodus **YeHoVaH** prepared for them. On Majestic wings is a wonderful place to travel as the living **YeHoVaH** carries a nation, a family, or a person to better ground.

To YeHoVaH **be the glory!**
Great things He has done!

PRINCIPLE # 21
The Power of Agreement (with believers)

Matthew 18: 19-20
> ¹⁹*Again I say unto you, That if two of you shall agree on earth as touching any thing that they shall ask, it shall be done for them of my Father which is in heaven.* ²⁰*For where two or three are gathered together in my name, there am I in the midst of them.*

When Sandra and I interceded together, we received the scripture verifying that Anthony would live. Although we never verbally said, "we agree together", the scripture we received held us in agreement with it and with each other. In addition, what I haven't yet mentioned is that believers at the church, informed of a desperate need for prayer, trusted **YeHoVaH** to move on Anthony's behalf. In short, believers were united in agreement that Anthony should live. **YeHoVaH**, help us not to forget the power of agreement with those of like faith!

THIS CHAPTER'S CONCLUSION
"Carried on Majestic Wings" is a wonderful example of an intercession that unites many *types* of intercession together. In this intercession, you have a combined use of:
- Situational Intercession (changing the circumstances while in progress)
- Substitute Intercession (seeing the intercessor as a stand in for an entire family)
- Transportational Intercession (making a pathway for the family to be carried)

There is also another type of intercession in use, but we won't discuss it until much later. I'll include it here, so you know, but don't worry about understanding right now. That type is

- Prophetic Intercession (establishing a prophetic pathway for **YeHoVaH**'s power to be released)

"Carried on Majestic Wings" is really an amazing witness to **YeHoVaH**'s Ability and the power of intercession. It is a marvellous example of the power of **YeHoVaH** to sustain an entire family during a trauma and rescue a young man from the jaws of death. Perhaps when you read this chapter, you wondered why this type of intercession didn't happen in a particular situation that you knew about.

People (saved and unsaved) of every age and in every nation constantly enter the jaws of death. Some are innocent victims of abductions or murders while others have been taken from this world by disease, accidents, or other horrible causes. Why does intercession not occur and change more situations? As I pondered this myself, I was reminded of a certain scripture passage:

Hebrews 11:32 to 40:
"32 ¶ And what shall I more say? for the time would fail me to tell of Gedeon, and of Barak, and of Samson, and of Jephthae; of David also, and Samuel, and of the

prophets: 33 Who through faith subdued kingdoms, wrought righteousness, obtained promises, stopped the mouths of lions, 34 Quenched the violence of fire, escaped the edge of the sword, out of weakness were made strong, waxed valiant in fight, turned to flight the armies of the aliens.

35 Women received their dead raised to life again: and others were tortured, not accepting deliverance; that they might obtain a better resurrection: 36 And others had trial of cruel mockings and scourgings, yea, moreover of bonds and imprisonment: 37 They were stoned, they were sawn asunder, were tempted, were slain with the sword: they wandered about in sheepskins and goatskins; being destitute, afflicted, tormented; 38 (Of whom the world was not worthy:) they wandered in deserts, and in mountains, and in dens and caves of the earth. 39 And these all, having obtained a good report through faith, received not the promise: 40 God having provided some better thing for us, that they without us should not be made perfect."

This scripture clearly states some believers received their promises, while others did not. Admittedly, this is a difficult passage to understand. Our human minds can't rationalize the difference, or how the choice is made either.

Likewise, we can't fully understand the choices in intercession either. We might conclude there are many things we will never understand this side of heaven, and intercession is one of those complex things, but we also might fit into our thinking the possibility that we need more intercessors and more in-depth training on intercession too.

As for an increase in intercessors and more in-depth intercession training, I am all for that. More intercessors are desperately needed, and I feel compelled to encourage every believer to seek the Face of **YeHoVaH** in this matter.

Whatever you do, don't settle back to receive whatever life dispenses, rather seek **YeHoVaH** in every situation to change what can be changed. Let us arise and be all we can be!

DEFINITION:
TRANSPORTATIONAL INTERCESSION

(Type A)
This word transport suggests a "carrying" process. In this type of intercession, **YeHoVaH** carries the intercessor as He will later carry other people over trauma, through storms, and other times of trouble. As a direct result, people are strengthened, encouraged, and carried over to the other side of an otherwise impossible situation or event in their life.

A WARRIOR FOR THE KINGDOM

An intercessor, although a go-between, is also a warrior for the Kingdom of **YeHoVaH**, packing power in the Name of Yeshua. Spiritual Warfare is inevitable for an intercessor, so be sure you enter battle wearing the armour of **YeHoVaH**. [24]

> *Ephesians 6: 10-18*
> [10]*Finally, my brethren, be strong in the Lord, and in the power of his might.* [11]*Put on the whole armour of God, that ye may be able to stand against the wiles of the devil.* [12]*For we wrestle not against flesh and blood, but against principalities, against powers, against the rulers of the darkness of this world, against spiritual wickedness in high places.* [13]*Wherefore take unto you*

---

[24] *Remember: it was soldiers that walked the wall!!!*

the whole armour of God, that ye may be able to withstand in the evil day, and having done all, to stand. ^{14}Stand therefore, having your loins girt about with truth, and having on the breastplate of righteousness; ^{15}And your feet shod with the preparation of the gospel of peace; ^{16}Above all, taking the shield of faith, wherewith ye shall be able to quench all the fiery darts of the wicked. ^{17}And take the helmet of salvation, and the sword of the Spirit, which is the word of God: ^{18}Praying always with all prayer and supplication in the Spirit, and watching thereunto with all perseverance and supplication for all saints;

Before entering battle, a good soldier wears protection and ensures their weapons are prepared and readily accessible. Our fight is against an adversary that is totally without scruples. Let us remember our weapons of warfare:

2 Corinthians 10: 3-6

^{3}For though we walk in the flesh, we do not war after the flesh: ^{4}(For the weapons of our warfare are not carnal, but mighty through God to the pulling down of strong holds;) ^{5}Casting down imaginations, and every high thing that exalteth itself against the knowledge of God, and bringing into captivity every thought to the obedience of

> Christ; ⁶*And having in a readiness to revenge all disobedience, when your obedience is fulfilled.*

Revelation 12: 10-11

> ¹⁰*And I heard a loud voice saying in heaven, Now is come salvation, and strength, and the kingdom of our God, and the power of his Christ: for the accuser of our brethren is cast down, which accused them before our God day and night.* ¹¹*And they overcame him by the <u>blood of the Lamb</u>, and by <u>the word of their testimony</u>; and <u>they loved not their lives unto the death</u>.*

There are also certain areas in our lives where protection is needed. Psalm 91 is an excellent Psalm to declare over your family, your business or ministry, your finances, and other such areas where ha satan might decide to attack.

Personally, I like to speak the Psalm directly to **YeHoVaH**, and put it in the first person. I declare this over my house, my family and any other areas needing protection.

Psalm 91: (Adjusted to first person)

I, <u>(name & all household)</u> dwell in the secret place of the most High God. I abide under the shadow of the Almighty. I say to you YeHoVaH, You are my refuge and my fortress: my God; in You will I trust. Without a doubt, You deliver me from every snare of the fowler, (every trap of the enemy) and from the noisome pestilence. You, YeHoVaH, cover me with Your feathers, and under Your wings I trust. Your truth is *my shield and buckler. Therefore, I am not afraid for the terror by night; nor for the arrow that flies by day; Nor for the pestilence that walks in darkness; nor for the destruction that wastes at noonday. A thousand shall fall at my side, and ten thousand at my right hand; but nothing comes near me.*

Only with my eyes shall I behold and see the reward of the wicked. Because I have made You, YeHoVaH, my refuge, even the most High, my habitation; No evil shall come near me, no plague, sickness, disease, or epidemic shall come near by home. For You, YeHoVaH give Your angels charge over me, to keep me in all my ways. They shall bear me up in their hands, so I won't cut my foot on any stone. I tread upon the lion and adder: the young lion and the dragon I trample under my feet. Because I fixed my love upon You, YeHoVaH, therefore You deliver me and set me on high because I have known Your Name. I call upon You and You answer me, YeHoVaH. You are with me in trouble; You deliver me and honour me. With a long life you satisfy me, and show me Your salvation.

Of course, your Heavenly Prayer Partner will do all that is declared in the above Psalm, and He will stand watch over every area of your life, with you. You can expect your covenant partner to "walk the walls on your life" [25]with you, warning of areas in need of an extra watch.

---

[25] *In the section called "Walking the Wall", this is explained further.*

In all things, remember

Romans 8: 35-39
> *³⁵Who shall separate us from the love of Christ? shall tribulation, or distress, or persecution, or famine, or nakedness, or peril, or sword? ³⁶As it is written, For thy sake we are killed all the day long; we are accounted as sheep for the slaughter. ³⁷Nay, in all these things we are more than conquerors through him that loved us. ³⁸For I am persuaded, that neither death, nor life, nor angels, nor principalities, nor powers, nor things present, nor things to come, ³⁹Nor height, nor depth, nor any other creature, shall be able to separate us from the love of God, which is in Christ Jesus our Lord.*

As a warrior, never forget you are called to be victorious, so do not shrink back from your assignments; go forward, knowing full well, as His child, you do not fight alone. Every battle is YeHoVaH's, and the victory is His gift to you, especially when you are partners with YeHoVaH for the advancement of the Kingdom of **YeHoVaH**!

INTO THE REALMS OF GLORY

When I was in my living room interceding for the nations, the Spirit suddenly carried me away into the heavenlies and put me down in the middle of an intense battle. To my left, I could see an army of soldiers on white horses moving rapidly towards adversary lines. Each soldier was dressed in a white robe with a narrow gold sash extending from the right shoulder, crossing the chest, and fastened at the waist. Bravely, they rode into battle to face the fierce army of horses and riders that stood against them.

By the Spirit of YeHoVaH, I knew there was great urgency about this battle. Opposing adversary forces stood at the gate of a certain nation, determined to protect their territory. For a long time, due to their control, that nation had been veiled in darkness. Its people had been robbed of the light of the gospel, but now this wicked army would be defeated and their assignment from hell defused. This battle's outcome would set in place a freedom for the presentation of the Word of YeHoVaH in that nation and so end an era of great opposition and severe bondage. After the battle, the gate to the nation would be wide-open for the entrance of a great number of ambassadors of the gospel of Yeshua. They would impact that nation, preach YeHoVaH's freedom to its people and release YeHoVaH's blessings throughout the nation.

Watching the battle in full force in front of me, I noticed how quickly things were moving. While I didn't have time to fix my mind on every detail on the battlefield, I did notice that each soldier in the battle, on both sides, was united to their cause and totally sold out to their leader. At that point, having accessed the battle in my mind, knowing why I was there, YeHoVaH placed commands in my mouth. I opened my mouth and with His authority, spoke out every command He gave me.

I did not record the commands, since there was no time to do so, but the commands were Rhema words of scripture along with prophetic words imparted into the battle. Before a command would be released from my mouth, thunder would sound, and then immediately, the command would come. Word spoken shot from my mouth and became "lightning bolts". Each lightning bolt acted like "a forerunner" to the entire army of white-robed soldiers. Piercing with power for a great distance ahead of these soldiers, each lightning bolt penetrated deep into the adversary's ranks, hitting their defences, and scattering the soldiers. As each lightning bolt flashed and a heavenly thunder accompanied it, I heard loud cheers coming from those white-robed soldiers. They rejoiced for the "power given to man by the Saviour".

After a short span of time, perhaps five minutes or so, the commands ended. Just then, the army of white-robed soldiers raced forward to take the ground now made available to them. As I watched them ride with power into the doorway of that nation, I was whisked away from the battle scene and placed back in my living room.

This intercession is termed:
TRANSPORTATIONAL INTERCESSION
Type B

This form of Transportational Intercession wore a different face then Type A, where I was taken in my vehicle from one place to another. In this intercession, YeHoVaH lifted me up into another realm and showed me what transpired in the heavenlies over a certain nation. YeHoVaH's Spirit is not a theatrical person, so no transportation happens for the sake of showing His power. Each transport has a divine purpose, even if it is not immediately recognized by the intercessor.

People, according to the Bible, can be transported in two ways out of their surroundings:
- <u>Transported physically,</u> where one is completely removed from their previous surroundings and placed elsewhere.
- <u>Transported in the "spirit",</u> where one's body remains in place, but the spirit is taken elsewhere and/or made aware of another place.

Let's look at these two ways.

Transported physically: In "Carried on Majestic Wings", we explained how the apostle Philip, in the book of Acts, was taken in body from one place to another, and we discussed my transport while in intercession. In that experience, I, like Philip, was transported.

One moment I was in one place on a quiet road, and another moment, I arrived *safely* at another place miles down the road. As I reflect on that experience, the only indicators of what took place were the immediate change in location and the time factor.

Transported in the "spirit": where one's body remains in place, but the spirit is taken elsewhere and/or made aware of another place. Here is the scriptural precedence.

> 2 Corinthians 12: 1-4
> ¹*It is not expedient for me doubtless to glory. I will come to visions and revelations of the Lord.* ²*I knew a man in Christ above fourteen years ago, (whether in the body, I cannot tell; or whether out of the body, I cannot tell: God knoweth;) such an one caught up to the third heaven.* ³*And I knew such a man, (whether in the body, or out of the body, I cannot tell: God knoweth;)* ⁴*How that he was caught up into paradise, and heard unspeakable words, which it is not lawful for a man to utter*

In this experience of the apostle Paul, he was not sure whether he was caught up in the heavenlies in his body, or only in his spirit. In Transportational Intercession, when you are swept into the heavenlies, it is hard to tell if your body is there, in the heavenlies, or if just your spirit has travelled there, and your feet are still firmly planted on terra firma. In whatever way YeHoVaH desires to implement a transport, you are safe in His Hands.

In this chapter, when I was plunked down in the middle of a heavenly battle, no matter how it raged, I had a sweet peace around me. Amazingly, I could feel the wind from the horses rushing by and heard the pounding, vibrating noise of horse's hoofs on the ground in front of me. Yet, in it all, there was no anxiety, only peace and a clear knowledge that YeHoVaH was very much in charge. He orchestrated everything, giving clear directions of what He expected of His intercessor. Trust and obey was all that was left to do!

THE BATTLE IN THE HEAVENLIES:

Most of the time, believers do not acknowledge battles in the heavenlies. Far too often believers focus only on what can be seen with human eyes, forgetting the spiritual realm we cannot see. We need reminders that we do not fight with flesh and blood, but rather with principalities and powers of darkness in heavenly places. Paul was very aware of battles in the heavenlies and considered the part the Ekklesia[26], plays in the battle.

Ephesians 3:7-12
> *⁷Whereof I was made a minister, according to the gift of the grace of God given unto me by the effectual working of his power. ⁸Unto me, who am less than the least of all saints, is this grace given, that I should preach among the Gentiles the unsearchable riches of Christ; ⁹And to make all men see what is the fellowship of the mystery, which from the beginning of the world hath*

---

[26] *Greek Word meaning the "called out ones" which we call the church*

> been hid in God, who created all things by Jesus Christ: ¹⁰*To the intent that now unto the principalities and powers in heavenly places might be known by the church the manifold wisdom of God,* ¹¹*According to the eternal purpose which he purposed in Christ Jesus our Lord:* ¹²*In whom we have boldness and access with confidence by the faith of him.*

As Paul preached the gospel, the Gentiles would receive the unsearchable riches of Messiah, *but* his message would also affect the heavenlies. *"¹⁰To the intent that now unto the principalities and powers in heavenly places might be known by the church the manifold wisdom of* YeHoVaH.*"* Although Paul spread the gospel to kings and magistrates, *the human beings in power*, he understood that the *spiritual adversary ruling in the heavenlies* would hear a message to reinforce Messiah's victory, a victory so complete it conquered them and the territory they possessed. In this manner, *the church* (Ekklesia or called out ones) demonstrates the manifold wisdom of YeHoVaH.

Rulers of nations, magistrates, and the like, can be pawns in the hands of satanic forces and while the human vessels may be the physical expression to the ideals of the kingdom of darkness affecting the kingdom of man, none of them, human or spiritual, have the last say. Messiah's victory ensures ultimate and total authority over every kingdom, including the kingdom of darkness that seeks to rule earthly kingdoms.

As we use the power in Messiah to push back adversary forces, we enter the spiritual battleground in the heavenlies, and by virtue of Messiah's death, we are given the victory. We proclaim and reinforce YeHoVaH's victory and the adversary's defeat. In other words, we wage war in *the heavenlies*. When we ignore this battle or refuse to acknowledge it, we abdicate our call to demonstrate the manifold wisdom of YeHoVaH. If we do not fight the battle in the heavenlies, the adversary will advance to oppress, deceive, and eventually snuff out anyone and everyone, anywhere and everywhere throughout the universe.

We must not allow the adversary to blind us to the existence of principalities and powers that constantly fight over people's lives, families, cities, regions, or nations. They must experience Messiah's authority to render them inoperative as we take back territories they have possessed, perhaps for centuries. We have the privilege to re-enforce Messiah's victory in the earth. On one hand, we battle the spiritual forces of darkness to enforce Messiah's victory, and on the other hand, we speak the gospel bringing Good News to all humanity.

**We must realize our dual role, and
then perform it.**

ANALYSIS OF THIS INTERCESSION

TRANSPORTATIONAL INTERCESSION, TYPE B

Once again, we will review the Principles of Intercession previously learned, and unless a principle is not too obvious, it will not be explained, only acknowledged.

EARLIER PRINCIPLES OF INTERCESSION

1.	YeHoVaH initiated the intercession. (Yes)
2.	Wait on YeHoVaH for His Leading & Guidance. (Yes)
3.	The Holy Spirit partnered with the believer. (Yes)
4.	The focus was shifted from the situation to YeHoVaH & His ability. (Yes)
5.	Agreement was made with YeHoVaH. (Yes)
6.	YeHoVaH's promises from the Word used as reminders to see them fulfilled and was declared into the situation to change it. (Yes)
7.	Intercession was made in the direct will of YeHoVaH through "groaning". (No)
8.	Intercession was made to YeHoVaH through weeping. (No)
9.	Intercession transpired until a peace came.
Yes	*In this case, the intercession began when I entered the heavenlies and ended when I was taken back to my home with a peace it was done.*

	10.	Assurance was given by YeHoVaH that intercession was complete.
Yes		*The objective to make a clear pathway to advance the gospel was completed, reassuring me "my part" in that matter had been finished.*
	11.	YeHoVaH gave words of knowledge.
Yes		*YeHoVaH did this when I knew what the battle was about.*
	12.	The vision was prayed into.
No vision		*This was a transport, with similar earmarks to a vision.*
	13.	YeHoVaH responded to the desperate cry.
Yes		*The need of the nation for salvation.*
	14.	The angels of YeHoVaH were sent into the situation. (No)
	15.	YeHoVaH broke off the dangerous thinking.
No		*Although perhaps indirectly*
	16.	Demonic Spiritual forces commanded to let go. (Yes)
	17.	YeHoVaH saw the intercessor as a substitute for another. (No)
	18.	YeHoVaH enacted a Divine Siege. (No)
	19.	YeHoVaH revealed hidden information. (Yes)
	20.	YeHoVaH initiated a transportation. (Yes)
	21.	The Power of Agreement with believers. (No)

NEW PRINCIPLES OF INTERCESSION

Let's look at what New Principles of Intercession were operative in "Into the Realms of Glory".

PRINCIPLE # 22

Agreement is made with
YeHoVaH's Plans and Purposes

In various places in this book, we have mentioned the importance of YeHoVaH's plans and our agreement with them. Here we will define it as a principle.

1 John 5:7 -9
> [7]*For there are three that bear record in heaven, the Father, the Word, and the Holy Ghost: and these three are one.* [8]*And there are three that bear witness in earth, the Spirit, and the water, and the blood: and these three agree in one.* [9]*If we receive the witness of men; the witness of God is greater: for this is the witness of God which he hath testified of his Son*

Things *in heaven* agree: *The Father, The Word, and the Holy Ghost;* and things *on earth*: *The Water, the Blood, and the Spirit.*

This is not a casual agreement that we are given here. To walk in such complete unity, agreeing every way, there must also be a complete unity in accomplishing plans and purposes.

Amos 3: 3
   ³Can two walk together, except they be agreed?

As Christians, we are called to agree with YeHoVaH (Principle # 5). As an intercessor, that agreement must be active and moving in the same direction as YeHoVaH. Only as we surrender our total being to YeHoVaH's control can we ever hope to always walk arm and arm with YeHoVaH in this manner. As we walk more with YeHoVaH we learn to trust Him more. That trust causes a greater yielding. That greater yielding to YeHoVaH, causes a greater walk, arm in arm with Him.

Although this is a process throughout our Christian life, somehow it magnifies in importance when in intercession. An intercessor can't afford to cling to any plans or human agendas of their own. They cannot have a purpose in mind other than the Lord's. To do so is to pull the intercession off target or miss the "bull's eye" altogether. Total dependence on **YeHoVaH** every step of the way and total agreement to His plans and Purposes is paramount.

To have success in intercession, we must fully agree with YeHoVaH without disputing His Plans, nor adding in our own ideas. Whether we know YeHoVaH's full plan, perceive only a small part or absolutely know nothing at all His plans, still we must stand in agreement. We can do this based on:

Jeremiah 29: 11:
¹¹For I know the thoughts that I think toward you, saith YeHoVaH, thoughts of peace, and not of evil, to give you an expected end.

As YeHoVaH's character builds in our understanding, we trust in His integrity, and in His ultimate perfect desire and care for us. When in intercession, we can agree with the Plans and Purposes of YeHoVaH, because we know they are for the benefit of all concerned, are without devious or selfish intent on the part of YeHoVaH and will bring Him honour and glory.

THIS CHAPTER'S CONCLUSION

"Into the Realms of Glory" was a Transportational Intercession that took place quickly and lasted for only a few minutes. Its primary purpose was to release YeHoVaH's orders into a heavenly battle that was in motion, but I believe it had a secondary purpose: to help intercessors (as well as others) become aware of the battles that transpire in the heavenly realms. These battles affect the world in which we live. We must be aware of them as we intercede for others. Our involvement *in spiritual battles* is part and parcel of our intercession, and to release such *authority in Messiah* is a blessing that brings Him great honour and glory, *on earth*, and in heaven.

While YeHoVaH transports the intercessor into the heavenlies, He is also capable of transporting the intercessor to different places on the earth, or over the earth. He simply lifts the intercessor from the place they are, then places them where He wants them. Every aspect of the intercession is released, and when the intercession is completed, YeHoVaH returns the intercessor to the place where the intercession began.

Once again, every form of intercession, including Transportational Intercession, will have a plan and a purpose. If the intercessor trusts YeHoVaH and does not limit His expressions of intercession, there will be tremendous activities in this realm beyond the intercessor's wildest dreams. YeHoVaH is a mighty **YeHoVaH** with a wonderful plan for the whole earth.

"Thy Kingdom Come in the earth, Oh Lord! Thy will be done!"

DEFINITION:
 <u>TRANSPORTATIONAL INTERCESSION</u>
 (Type B)
This word "transport" suggests a carrying process. In this type of intercession, YeHoVaH carries the intercessor into the heavenlies, elsewhere on the earth, or even over the earth. While in the heavenlies, the

intercessor is there for a specific purpose, whether it is to give orders to a raging battle or to make proclamations of a prophetic nature into situations on the earth or fulfill some other purpose. As a-result an event, situation or perhaps even a nation's history changes. Only heaven reveals all the effects!

KEEP FOCUSED ON YEHOVAH:

An intercessor should not measure their success, as such, by any measured amount of intercession or any type experienced either. The plain truth in the matter is this: *it is YeHoVaH's call on an intercessor's life that will lead them to any supernatural experience, and it will be to fulfill His Purpose.* Intercessors have nothing to do with this, other than being a yielded vessel. Anyone YeHoVaH *commissions* to do anything for Him will always find that the miraculous must be done with intent to bring YeHoVaH Praise, Honour and Glory, and for no other reason. It is no different with intercession. No merit belongs to the intercessor, only YeHoVaH. An intercessor must always keep their mind fixed on YeHoVaH and nothing else, and always, give Him the glory.

!

MORE ABOUT INTERCESSION

These stories of intercession from my life[27] just touch the tip of the iceberg on intercession. So much more awaits the diligent and obedient intercessor who willing follows the leading of the Holy Spirit.

With these biblical principles fresh in your mind, get ready for Volume 2! This book brings out specific intercessions straight from the Bible. As you read them, as you explore them with a fresh viewpoint, your heart should rejoice at how much more you see now and understand since you know some basic principles of intercession!

---

[27] Which also included some intercessions from the Bible.

APPENDIX

APPENDIX

YeHoVaH[28]

Name to Honour

If, today, someone asked you to tell them the name of your earthly father, without hesitation you would declare it. If, for some reason, you did not know the identity of your earthly father, you would say so. You might even give an explanation as to why that might be so. Thus said, if asked to relate the name of your heavenly Father, today, would you do so with ease, or would you draw a blank?

Most of Christendom, today, is totally ignorant as to the name of the Father, as well as the way to pronounce it. As the author of this book, I would like to join the ranks of those who wish to relate that name to the world. When we stand before the Father on the day, we give an account for our deeds in this body, it would be a good thing to know Him, His Name and how it is pronounced!

---

[28] *Based on information given by Michael Rood. Some from his work entitled, The Chronological Bible, and some from his YouTube videos. For more information see page 28 of the Chronological Bible.*

Did you know that the name of the Father appears at least 6,828 times in the Hebrew scriptures? Scribes recorded it with four specific Hebrew letters. They are as follows:

י	Pronounced yode, or yod
ה	Pronounced as hey
ו	Pronounced as vav
ה	Pronounced as hey

For centuries, whenever the Jews come across these 4 letters they simply say, Adonai, or Ha Shem (meaning the name). They refuse to pronounce the name for several reasons, some of which we will look at momentarily. For now, let us look at whether their tradition affected Christianity. That we can easily do by looking at our Bibles to see the 4-letter name of the Father either written or substituted.

A quick look reveals that our KVJ Bibles, as well as many other versions, the 4-letter name presented to readers is a 4-letter English word, "LORD" [29]. Whether intentional or not, Christendom has followed the ancient tradition of the Jews.

AN ANCIENT TRADITION
In early second century times[30] Rabbis hid the pronunciation of the holy name of God. They did this by omitting the vowel pointings, which are necessary

---

[29] *In some translations it is GOD.*
[30] *Some scholars even dating further back.*

to make the name pronounceable. Hence, as they carefully wrote the scriptures, their omittance of the vowel pointings made the name unpronounceable. Historians believe there were two reasons why they did this:

1. According to Josephus, Rome, under the rule of Domitian, 81 to 96 CE, put to death anyone using the name of the Jewish or Christian God.
2. Many believe that the Rabbis borrowed a tradition from pagans, whereby the name of their god was considered too holy to mention, so they called him "Ba-al" meaning Lord. The Jews adopted this practice and most still practice it today, even some Messianic Jews!

TRADITION CONTINUES
Bible translators followed their tradition for many reasons which are not presently known. It is possible, they forgot the pronunciation of the name, but more than likely, those who knew it, hid it[31]. Whatever the reason, following this tradition caused Christians to continue in this tradition.

Does that tradition offend the Heavenly Father?

If indeed its origin was Baal worship, then we can give a resounding Amen to the fact it offends God. In

---

[31] *According to some, the Jews secretly knew the name.*

addition, as we look at scripture, we see the Almighty was not pleased with this, for His Heart desires all to enjoy salvation, including the Gentiles. How can that happen if they do not know upon what name they should call? Scripture[32] clearly says in the end times, Gentiles will know His name and call upon it to receive salvation. Obviously, for that to happen, they must know the name of YeHoVaH ((יְהֹוָה)).

AN HISTORIC DISCOVERY
Today, some Hebrew scholars[33] have searched the world over for Hebrew manuscripts. In doing so, they found many Hebrew documents have the full name with vowels and therefore the pronunciation of the name. These scholars may different slightly in pronunciation, but nevertheless, they are making the name of YeHoVaH known today.

OUR SAVIOUR'S NAME
In looking at the Hebrew root of the name of the Father, pronounced *Yah-Ho **Vah'***, and looking at another scripture, we see something amazing about our Saviour. In speaking of the Prophet, the one the

---

[32] *Jeremiah 16:1-21 The word of YeHoVaH came also unto me, saying, 2 Thou shalt not take thee a wife, neither shalt thou have sons or daughters in this place.*

[33] *Nehemiah Gordon, a Hebrew scholar, according to his testimony, found the name of the Father with all vowel pointings in the Aleppo Codex, and through his efforts and those of others discovered that name with vowels pointings in over 2000 manuscripts.*

Father would send and to whom all must listen and obey, YeHoVaH said that His name would be in the name of the Prophet.

Exodus 23:21 "Beware of him, and obey his voice, provoke him not; for he will not pardon your transgressions[34]: *for my name [is] in him.*"

Our Saviour's name, as given by the angel was "Yehoshua", which means Salvation.

That name, with its Hebrew letters reads as:

י	Pronounced yode or yod
ה	Pronounced hey
ו	Pronounced vav
שׁ	Pronounced shin
ע	Pronounced ayin

The name of the Father (יְהֹוָה) is in the name of the Son! The first three letters of YeHoVaH show it! (Yod, Heh, Vav). Is it so amazing that the name of our Father is in the true name of the One YeHoVaH sent to redeem us!

HONOUR THE FATHER'S NAME

Throughout this book, and all later books, as well as all accompanying audios and PowerPoints, it is the

---

[34] *Please keep in mind that Yeshua bore the punishment for your sins. Your sins were not pardoned, they were atoned!*

author's intention to widely use, proclaim and continually pronounce the name of the Father, as well as the name of Yeshua. Indeed, this breaks with tradition of many, however, thus far as we have shared the news of the Father's name and use Yeshua's birth name, reception has been excellent.

NAME CHALLENGE

Since, as of this reading, you are no longer ignorant of your heavenly Father's name, we invite you to join the unofficial network of proclaimers of the Father's name and shout it from the house tops. In doing so, you honour the Heavenly Father, our Savour Yeshua, and the Holy Spirit.

ABOUT THE KING JAMES VERSION

Scriptures quoted in this book *originate* from the KJV **public domain version** of the Bible, which means, no copyright exists on this version of the scripture. While some find this translation outdated, Jeanne, trained in the KJV still finds this version helpful, and uses it in all her books[35].

In using KJV, however, it is good to remember the following:

- Some words in the KJV have changed meaning over the centuries. To understand such words, look up the root word in its original language. In doing so, the meaning stands out. For example. KJV uses the word "conversation" however, in its original language it means moral character, or behaviour.
- When KJV spoke of humanity, they said, "man". When you read that word, or hear others speak about the scriptures using the term, "man", know it refers to all humankind, not a specific gender.

Due to tradition, the name of the Father, YeHoVaH appears as LORD, or at times as Jehovah. However, in all Jeanne's manuscripts, YeHoVaH's name replaces the term LORD. To learn more read "A Name to Honour", located in the Appendix section.

---

[35] In later manuscripts, the author updated the more archaic words in the KJV such as wouldest or couldest.

REMEMBER:
NO FORMULAS FOR SUCCESS

- The following principles are not to be used as a formula. We have patterns for prayer in the Word such as "The Lord's Prayer", but no formulas are given to us. Solutions to problems resolved through intercession are just as creative and unique as the problem itself.
- There may be similarities in the circumstances but a rigid approach that uses identical principles each time does not exist.
- In every intercession, there will be **"uncertain ingredients"** that only YeHoVaH can reveal. With the Wisdom of YeHoVaH, a person can build upon the principles they learn, but these are only keys to open the door to understanding how intercession operates.

JONAH'S SITUATIONAL INTERCESSION

In the chapter entitled, "The Shocking Reality of Visions", a reference was made to Jonah's situational intercession (Jonah 2: 1-10). In that chapter, you were asked to consider analyzing that intercession to pick out certain principles of intercession. On the following pages you will find my list of principles, which you can use to compare to yours...

JONAH'S INTERCESSION

In Chapter 3, you looked at Jonah's intercession. Below, you'll find a review of principles found in that intercession. See how many you discovered on your own!

	Its application in *Jonah 2:1-10* **PRINCIPLES 1-14**
1.	**YeHoVaH initiated the intercession.**
Yes	*Jonah was positioned in a situation that required him to face His God and intercede for his own life. The Lord prepared the storm, (and calmed it immediately after Jonah was removed from the sailing vessel) and the Lord prepared the big fish as well. In my opinion, the Sovereign Hand of the Almighty set the scene for this intercession, thus initiating it.*
2.	**Wait on YeHoVaH for His Leading and Guidance.**
Yes	*Jonah's prayer was centered into the will of YeHoVaH, which is evidenced by its fulfillment. It takes the leading and guidance of the Holy Spirit to hit the center*

	of YeHoVaH's will. Jonah was in the fish for three days and nights (Jonah 1:17). What went on between Jonah and the Lord we are not told, but Jonah's intercession is scripture. To classify as scripture, every word must be inspired by the Holy Spirit. That does not happen without the Lord's leading or guidance.
3.	**The Holy Spirit partnered with the believer.**
Yes	*The same logic as above applies to this point. The Holy Spirit had to partner with Jonah, or else you would not have a record of scripture here. In addition, the prayer was centered into the will of* YeHoVaH, *which again, takes the help of the Holy Spirit.*
4.	**The focus was shifted from the situation to YeHoVaH and His ability.**
Yes	*As you read Jonah, Chapter 2, verses 3 to 7, you can see Jonah's transition from focusing on his situation to the Lord's greatness.*
5.	**Agreement was made with YeHoVaH.**
Yes	*Vs 3 clearly shows agreement as Jonah recognizes the Hand of the Lord at work, and his own actions that caused the situation. In verse 9 of chapter 2, Jonah*

	6.	*shows his agreement that salvation comes from YeHoVaH.* **YeHoVaH's Promises from the Word used as reminders to see them fulfilled and YeHoVaH's Word was spoken into the Situation.**
Yes		*Jonah, in verse 9, promises to pay his vows. This promise Jonah could not be realized unless* the Lord *changed the situation and gave him life in place of death. Jonah's faith and hope were highly active here, holding to* the Lord *fulfilling the promise. Many parts of Jonah's prayer contain scripture. In verse 5, Jonah quotes Psalm 42:7 almost word for word. "All thy billows and thy waves passed over me." David recorded it earlier, in a prophetic sense, but Jonah saw it fulfilled, that moment, in his life.*

7.	Intercession was made in the direct will of YeHoVaH through groaning.
?	We are not told this happened, but it is possible.
8.	Intercession is made to YeHoVaH through weeping.
Not known	Again, this is not specifically mentioned but again, it is possible.
9.	Intercession transpired until a peace came.
Yes	In Chapter 2: 6 Jonah declares: "the earth with her bars was about me forever, yet thou has brought up my life from corruption, O Lord my God." This statement precedes his statement to offer sacrifice, paying what he had vowed. It is possible that Jonah had both a peace and an assurance, which gave him such confidence to know he would again see land. However, the peace and assurance are not clearly stated.
10.	Assurance was given by YeHoVaH that the intercession was complete.
Yes	See point above
11.	YeHoVaH gave a word of knowledge.
?	As in point # 9, the knowledge that he be able to keep his vow, may have come by a word of knowledge, giving him peace and assurance.
12.	The vision was prayed into.
No	This does not apply here.

	13.	**YeHoVaH responded to the desperate cry.**
Yes		*The Lord certainly did respond to Jonah's desperate cry.*
	14.	**The angels of YeHoVaH were sent into the situation.**
No		*This principle was not used here.*

PRINCIPLES OF INTERCESSION BY NUMBER AS TAUGHT FROM VOLUME 1

#	Description (Principles put into "present tense".)
1	YeHoVaH initiates the intercession
2	The Intercessor Waits on YeHoVaH for His Leading and Guidance
3	The Holy Spirit partners with the believer
4	The focus shifts from the situation to YeHoVaH & His ability
5	Agreement is made with *YeHoVaH*
6	YeHoVaH's promises from the Word are used as reminders so they can see their fulfillment; and YeHoVaH's Word is spoken into the Situation to change the direction of the event.
7	Intercession is made in the direct will of YeHoVaH through "groaning"
8	Intercession is made in the direct will of YeHoVaH through weeping
9	Intercession transpires until a peace comes
10	Assurance is given by YeHoVaH, that the intercession is complete
11	YeHoVaH gives a word (s) of knowledge
12	The vision is prayed into
13	YeHoVaH responds to the desperate cry

14	The angels of YeHoVaH are sent into the situation
15	YeHoVaH breaks off any dangerous thinking
16	Demonic Spiritual Forces are commanded to let go
17	YeHoVaH sees the Intercessor as a Substitute
18	YeHoVaH enacts a Divine Siege
19	YeHoVaH reveals hidden information
20	YeHoVaH brings about a transport
21	Power of Agreement is made with other Believers
22	Agreement is made with YeHoVaH's Plans and Purposes

(Volume 2 shows these principles operative in further intercessions and introduces some new principles as well!)

INTERCESSORY TYPES DEFINED in Volume 1:

There are various definitions regarding intercession and what transpires during intercession. This book does not claim to be an exhaustive source of the types of intercession but rather shares certain aspects of intercession, defining types to generally summarize what is presented in this book.

GROANING & WEEPING INTERCESSION[36]

Groaning and Weeping Intercession is a powerful form of intercession that comprises an entire intercession. Groans *(unutterable sounds)* and/or "weeping" *(even as YeHoVaH did with loud cries)* are released **by the Holy Spirit** through the vessel, *(the believer)* directly into the center of YeHoVaH's will. This happens to bring His Power into a situation. This kind of intercession usually operates where human knowledge is inadequate. At times, the intercessor may not know the reason for "weeping and groaning" style intercession and may not understand what "fruit" it has brought forth. Nevertheless, since the Holy Spirit births it, eternal results are produced, accomplishing what human beings could never have done alone.

---

[36] Groaning & Weeping can also be a principle of intercession.

SITUATIONAL INTERCESSION

This intercession takes place while a situation is *in progress*. The Holy Spirit directs the intercession with specific intentions *to change* the situation as it happens. Intercession is made until the situation is re-aligned to the plans and purposes of YeHoVaH. It may or may not bear the marks of YeHoVaH's intervention.

PREVENTATIVE INTERCESSION

This intercession transpires <u>*before*</u> an incident occurs. Due to the changes brought about through preventative intercession, an event may appear in a reduced status, or it may manifest differently than originally shown to the intercessor. There may be traces of the event showing the background activities that led up to the event, or even these may be eliminated, so no trace of the event is evidenced at all.

SUBSTITUTE INTERCESSION

As a type of intercession, Substitute Intercession carries out, through the power of the Holy Spirit, the biblical principle for *substitution* throughout *the entire intercession* and enables an intercessor to be seen, in the eyes of YeHoVaH, as a substitute for someone else. Manifestations, like the person in need, may be superimposed upon the intercessor, who in turn uses their own knowledge of Scripture and of the benefits of the cross to bring victory into the situation as they complete the intercession.

TRANSPORTATIONAL INTERCESSION TYPE A
The word transport suggests a "carrying" process. In this type of intercession, YeHoVaH carries the intercessor, as He will later carry other people over trauma, through storms, and other times of trouble. As a direct result, people are strengthened, encouraged, and carried over to the other side of an otherwise, impossible situation or event in their life.

TRANSPORTATIONAL INTERCESSION TYPE B: The word transport suggests a carrying process. In this type of intercession, YeHoVaH carries the intercessor into the heavenlies, or elsewhere on the earth, or even over the earth. While in the heavenlies, the intercessor is there for a specific purpose, whether it is to give orders to a raging battle or to make proclamations of a prophetic nature, into situations on the earth, or fulfill some other purpose. The end-result changes an event, situation or perhaps even a nation's history. Only heaven may reveal all the effects!

SALVATION'S MESSAGE

Yeshua, when walking on earth, said this:
John 3:14-18
> 14 And as Moses lifted up the serpent in the wilderness, even so must the Son of man be lifted up: 15 That whosoever believes in him should not perish but have eternal life. 16 For God so loved the world, that he gave his only begotten Son, that whosoever believes in him should not perish, but have everlasting life. 17 For God sent not his Son into the world to condemn the world; but that the world through him might be saved. 18 He that believes on him is not condemned: but he that believes not is condemned already, because he hath not believed in the name of the only begotten Son of God.

During the time of Moses, the children of Israel, in the wilderness, rebelled against God, at which time poisonous serpents infiltrated the camp, killing many of the people. After seeking YeHoVaH for a solution to the problem, Moses followed God's instructions and made a bronze serpent fashioned and erected it on a pole in sight of the people. Whosoever wanted to live, must acknowledge their rebellion against YeHoVaH, and in doing so, look upon the erected pole and bronze serpent, to YeHoVaH, who gave them life in place of death, then they would live.

Yeshua said, just as Moses erected that bronze serpent in the wilderness, He would be lifted for all to see. This referred to the event, in the future, of Yeshua's crucifixion. During the time when the serpent hung on that pole, whosoever wanted to live and not die from the serpent's bite must acknowledge their rebellion, their sin against YeHoVaH.

Likewise, for those who wish to live eternally, they must look upon the cross of the crucified One, to YeHoVaH, who provided life for them. This was an act of love for all humankind, necessary because man is born from Adam, and thus is born with an inherent sin.

Secondly, man sins. The consequence of sin is death, and eternal death, wherein man will spend an eternity in darkness, away from YeHoVaH. Unfortunately, there is nothing humanly possible to reverse those consequences. Even if a person had made a genuine decision never to sin again, and for some reason they succeeded, all their good deeds and good living would not erase the penalty of eternal death.

There is only *one way* for Eternal Life to touch a person's life. That is the way Yeshua explained to His listeners, *through the works done by God on the cross.*

Salvation comes by understanding these facts:
1. Yeshua, being the Son of God and the fulfilment of the scriptures, never sinned.
2. YeHoVaH, on behalf of every human being on the earth, chose to make Yeshua become as sin, in His Eyes, so that Yeshua might pay the penalty for sin, for all of humanity.
3. Yeshua paid that penalty. He died on the cross and was buried in a tomb.
4. Three days later, He rose again, appearing to His disciples, to show them the reality of His resurrection, to show them God vindicated Him and made Him both Lord and Messiah.
5. Yeshua could not stay in the tomb, because "death" comes to all who sin, but since Yeshua never sinned, therefore, death could not hold Him in the grave.
6. All those who come to Yeshua, to receive Him as their Saviour, receive liberty from sin and from its horrible consequence, eternal death.
7. They enter YeHoVaH's Kingdom and receive eternal life, as well as another gift: **The Righteousness of Messiah.** After salvation, when YeHoVaH looks upon a believer in Messiah, He sees Yeshua's perfect life and sees a redeemed believer, set aside for YeHoVaH. Since salvation has taken place in the believer, the Holy Spirit dwells within them.
8. All it takes to receive salvation from YeHoVaH is receiving His Messiah, fully repenting from sinning

against God[37]. YeHoVaH even gives the believer the faith to receive His gift of Salvation!

The Apostle Paul put it this way:
Ephesians 2:8
"For by grace are ye saved through faith; and that not of yourselves: it is the gift of God"

When you pray the following prayer, realize we present it here to get you started in your walk with YeHoVaH. Living out your salvation depends upon your commitment to follow through *from this point, onward*. From the moment of your commitment and onward, dear one, please seek YeHoVaH for His help in all things, including help to make your life align with truth, and in the end be a praise unto His name, forever!

SINNER'S PRAYER
& LIFETIME COMMITMENT

Heavenly, Father:
    I acknowledge before You, Lord, that I am a sinner.
    I understand sin's punishment is a life without You, for all eternity. Thank You for sending Yeshua to the earth, as the Messiah. I understand now that He died in my place, to take my punishment for my

---

[37] And against man. When a person steals, etc. they sin against both God and man. PLEASE NOTE: all references to "man", either by scripture or the author, refers to all humankind, not a specific gender.

sins. I believe You raised Yeshua from the dead, and now that I've I accepted Him as my personal Saviour, my old life dies, and my new life begins.

I humbly ask You, Lord, to forgive me of my sins, and as of this moment, I receive Yeshua as my Mashiach. I open my heart to receive the works of the cross that You provided for me through Yeshua, and with Your help, I will walk away from my sin, turning my back upon my own will and ways. I will now live my life seeking to obey Your Word and Your will. Help me to live, from this point onward, in a manner pleasing to You.

One more thing:

Remember, this gospel message comes with power. When you hear it, the Kingdom of God draws near to you. When you repent of your sins and receive Salvation, the Kingdom of God moves within. You cannot see it, feel it, or tell it from an outward observance. It is accepted, received, and lived out by faith! Seek out other believers in Messiah and may God bless you richly as you live your live, now, completely for Him!

So now, be sure and tell someone!

Remember that a person believes with the heart unto righteousness and confesses with their mouth unto salvation, as spoken about in *Romans 10:10*:

10 For with the heart man believes unto righteousness; and with the mouth confession is made unto salvation

SCRIPTURE INDEX

1

1 Corinthians 12:8 78
1 John 3:8 135
1 John 5:14-15 63
1 John 5:7 -9 189

2

2 Corinthians 10: 3-6 . 175
2 Corinthians 12: 1-4 183

A

Acts 10:3 14
Acts 12: 5-11 82
Acts 16: 30-31 160
Acts 16:31 155
Acts 26:31 56
Acts 8:39-40 146
Amos 3: 3 190

C

Chapter 2: 6 208

D

Daniel 2:22 81
Deuteronomy 29:29 .. 136
Deuteronomy 7: 22-24
.... 138

E

Ephesians 1:17-23 87
Ephesians 2:8 ...... 48, 218
Ephesians 3:7-12 184
Ephesians 6: 10-18 174
Ephesians 6:12 92
Exodus 19: 4 169
Exodus 23:21 201
Exodus 32:9-14 ...... 39, 98
Ezekiel 22: 30 41

G

Genesis 18:16-32 37
Genesis 18:16-33 96
Genesis 22:11-14 123
Genesis 22:5 122
Genesis 22:9-12 . 121, 122

H

Hebrews 11:32 to 40 . 171
Hebrews 5:7 59

I

Isaiah 14:27 106
Isaiah 29: 1-4 133
Isaiah 55: 11 165
Isaiah 59: 16 41

J

Jeremiah 16:1-2 200
Jeremiah 23: 29 165
Jeremiah 29: 11 191
Job 15:11b 136
Jonah 1:17 206
Jonah 2: 1-10 .... 73, 205
Jonah 2:1-10 205

L

Luke 10:19 108
Luke 18:19 42
Luke 22:41-43 82

M

Matthew 12: 43-45 ... 139
Matthew 16:19[b] 107

Matthew 18: 19-20 ... 170

P

Philippians 4: 6 60
Psalm 118:17 150
Psalm 18: 5-6 81
Psalm 42:7 207
Psalm 9: 1-4 94

R

Revelation 12: 10-11 . 176
Revelation 12: 11 109
Revelation 5: 12 b 161
Romans 1:17 48
Romans 10:10: 219
Romans 8: 26- 27 57
Romans 8: 35-39 178
Romans 8:26-27 .... 32, 57

OTHER BOOKS BY THIS AUTHOR (as of 2022)

Bible Studies textbook and workbook sold separately. Devotionals present scripture for thought and give room to record your personal comments.

Note: the book is a Bible Study unless other wise marked.

An Arsenal of Powerful Prayers [38]
   Scriptural Prayers to Move Mountains (Prayer book)

Arising Incense
   A Believer's Priesthood Watching

Candidate for A Miracle
   Wisdom from the miracles of Yeshua

Foundations of Revival
   Biblical Evidence for Revival

His Reflection
   What God longs to see in His People

Heaven's Greater Government
   Behind the Scenes of Earth's Events

In The Name of Yehovah We Set Up Our Banners
   Biblical use of banners

It's All About Heaven
   As Pictured in Scripture

Kingdom Keys for Kingdom Kids
   Walking in Kingdom Power

Molded for the Miraculous
   Why God made You

---

[38] *This is a book of written prayers of various topics to help believers live a stronger, active faith. No workbook.*

Releasing the Impossible
The Limitless Power of Intercession
Volume 1: Intercessions in Action
Volume 2: Intercessions from Biblical Characters

Salvation Depicted in a Meal [39]
A Hebraic Christian Guide to Passover
This is a Haggadah.

The Jeremiah Generation
God's Response to Injustice

The Warrior Bride-
God's Kingdom Advancing through Spiritual Warfare

Thy Kingdom Come
Entering God's Rest in Prayer

Watching, Waiting, Warning
Obeying Yeshua's Command to Watch & Pray
Comes with 1 textbook, 1 workbook, 1 prayer book.

When Nations Rumble
A Study of the Book of Amos

Worship in Spirit and In Truth [40]
The Tabernacle of David - Past, Present & Future

By Year End 2022, it is Cegullah's goal to have all these wonderful studies, plus a devotional series, available for purchase online. To keep updated check Amazon or Cëgullah Publishing.

---

[39] *Haggadah (Guide) for a Christian Passover. No Workbook.*
[40] *Good sister book to "In the Name of YeHoVaH we set up our banners".*

ABOUT THE AUTHOR

Jeanne Metcalf has served YeHoVaH for over forty years. Presently, she serves in the capacity of an ordained minister, working as the Senior Pastor of a ministry, named *"Forward March!"* Ministries (FMM). FMM is a part of a global grassroots movement of the Holy Spirit to return Christianity to its New Testament roots. Its primary goals include teaching early church concepts, spreading the gospel, and discipling believers so that all can walk in New Testament power, equipped to turn the world upside down with the impact of the gospel.

Jeanne gained credibility as a gifted teacher, writer, and speaker through her activities with FMM. With her passion for souls, a God-given insight and love for the Word of God, Rev. Jeanne presents sound biblical teachings on both the Hebraic and Apostolic scriptures, with clarity and simplicity, in a refreshing straightforward format. Those who study the Bible with Jeanne, highly recommend her studies.

Transformed lives stand as witnesses as through Rev. Jeanne's leadership, believers stand equipped, steadfast in their faith, prepared to live it out triumphantly.

To contact Jeanne, go to
www.cegullahpublishing.ca

www.ingramcontent.com/pod-product-compliance
Lightning Source LLC
Chambersburg PA
CBHW071157160426
43196CB00011B/2109